Early Views of India

The Picturesque Journeys of
Thomas and William Daniell
1786–1794

Early Views of India

The Picturesque Journeys of
Thomas and William Daniell
1786–1794

The Complete Aquatints

with 258 illustrations, 33 in colour and 3 maps

MILDRED ARCHER

T & H THAMES AND HUDSON

Acknowledgments

Thanks are due to the owners of pictures reproduced, who are mentioned in the captions, and, for allowing prints to be photographed in colour by John Webb, to Pauline Baines (*XI, XXX*), Messrs Eyre and Hobhouse, London (*V, X, XIII, XXIII, XXIV, XXVI, XXVIII, XXXI and XXXII*), and the India Office Library, London (*IV*). The black-and-white photographs of aquatints are all from the India Office Library.
Excerpts have been quoted from, and the Appendices partly based on, Thomas Sutton's *The Daniells: artists and travellers* (London, 1954), by kind permission of The Bodley Head.

On the title page
'The Great Bull, an Hindoo Idol, at Tanjore' (no. 124)

Colour illustrations originated in Switzerland by Cliché Lux SA, La Chaux de Fonds, and printed in Great Britain by Balding + Mansell Limited, Wisbech, Cambridgeshire
Filmset and printed in Great Britain by BAS Printers Limited, Over Wallop, Hampshire
Bound in Great Britain

Contents

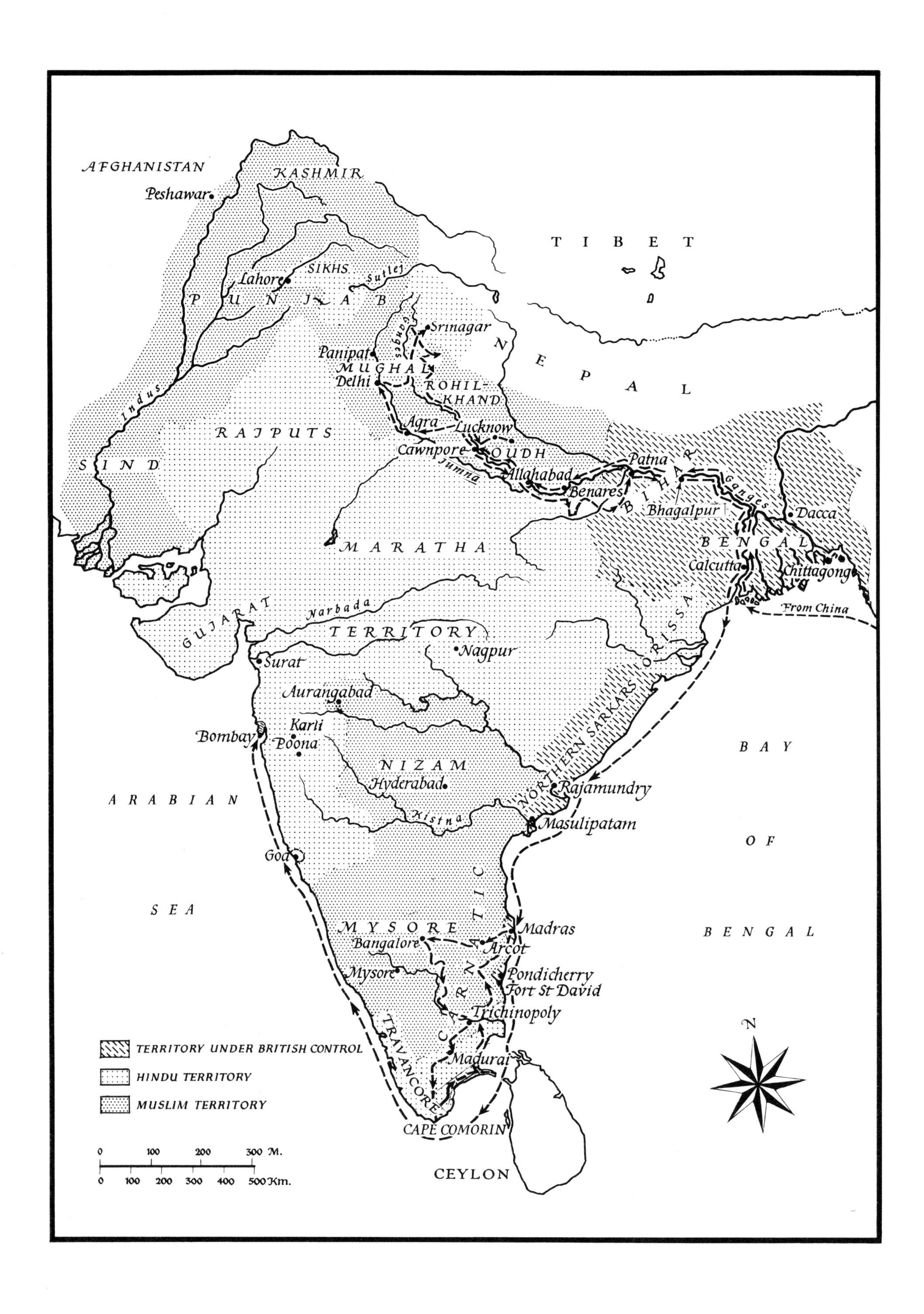
AFGHANISTAN
KASHMIR
Peshawar
TIBET
Lahore
SIKHS
Sutlej
PUNJAB
Srinagar
Ganges
Panipat
NEPAL
MUGHAL
Delhi
ROHIL-KHAND
Indus
Agra
Lucknow
RAJPUTS
Cawnpore
OUDH
SIND
Jumna
Patna
Allahabad
Benares
BIHAR
Bhagalpur
Ganges
Dacca
MARATHA
BENGAL
Calcutta
Chittagong
GUJARAT
Narbada
ORISSA
From China
TERRITORY
Nagpur
Surat
Aurangabad
Karli
Bombay
Poona
NORTHERN SARKARS
BAY
NIZAM
Hyderabad
Rajamundry
ARABIAN
Kistna
Masulipatam
OF
Goa
CARNATIC
SEA
Madras
BENGAL
MYSORE
Bangalore
Arcot
Pondicherry
Fort St David
Mysore
Trichinopoly
TRAVANCORE
N
TERRITORY UNDER BRITISH CONTROL
HINDU TERRITORY
MUSLIM TERRITORY
Madurai
CAPE COMORIN
0 100 200 300 M.
0 100 200 300 400 500 Km.
CEYLON

Science has had her adventurers, and philanthropy her achievements: the shores of Asia have been invaded by a race of students with no rapacity but for lettered relics; by naturalists, whose cruelty extends not to one human inhabitant; by philosophers, ambitious only for the extirpation of error, and the diffusion of truth. It remains for the artist to claim his part in these guiltless spoliations, and to transport to Europe the picturesque beauties of these favoured regions.

THOMAS AND WILLIAM DANIELL,
A Picturesque Voyage to India by the Way of China, 1810

Preface

THE AQUATINTS OF INDIA by Thomas and William Daniell have been continuously popular ever since their publication between 1795 and 1810. The British serving in India purchased them for their libraries or framed them for their houses, offices and clubs. In the early nineteenth century connoisseurs of art and architecture eagerly acquired them for their celebration of the 'sublime', the 'picturesque' and the 'exotic', as well as for their recording of antiquities. After Queen Victoria was proclaimed Empress of India in 1877 they were valued for their romantic depiction of the subcontinent – that 'jewel in the crown'. It is not surprising, therefore, that as a result of wear and tear and natural wastage an unbroken set of the six parts of *Oriental Scenery* or the smaller *A Picturesque Voyage to India by the Way of China* can rarely be found today. Even individual prints have become scarce and expensive. At the same time the work of the Daniells has gained a fresh popularity. Since the 1950s, air travel and the popularity of conducted tours has opened up India not only to a new generation of European travellers but to thousands of enlightened visitors from other continents. Many of these have been introduced to the work of the Daniells for the first time; and this interest has been reflected in a number of important exhibitions. Drawings and watercolours from the remarkable collection of the P & O Steam Navigation Company were shown at the Commonwealth Institute, London, in 1960, at the Smithsonian Institution, Washington, in 1962 and by Spink and Son, again in London, in 1974. The first *catalogue raisonné* of the oil paintings of Thomas and William Daniell, by Dr Maurice Shellim, was published in 1979. It is, however, the aquatints by these artists that are best known and most sought after by modest collectors.

It seems an appropriate time, therefore, to publish this book which reproduces all the aquatints of India engraved by the Daniells themselves from their own drawings. It also includes those engraved by Thomas Daniell after the watercolours of his friend, James Wales, who died in Western India before he could publish them himself. The reduced edition of *Oriental Scenery* (1812–16) and minor works, such as the few illustrations with Indian backgrounds in *Interesting Selections from Animated Nature* (1807–12), have been omitted: they are listed in Appendix I. Prints by other engravers after the Daniells are listed in Appendix II.

The illustrations have been arranged for the first time in the order of the Daniells' journeys, rather than in the order of publication of the aquatints. This arrangement helps to emphasize the pioneer character of the artists' travels, which were frequently through little-known areas. It may also encourage readers to visit India and themselves follow in the footsteps of the Daniells – something which with modern transport is perfectly feasible. In 1972 and

Map of India, showing the Daniells' journeys. From Calcutta they travelled north-west as far as Srinagar in the Himalayan foothills, then returned to Calcutta, partly by a different route (see the detailed map, pp. 44–45). After sailing to Madras, they made a circular journey down to Cape Comorin and back (map, p. 189). Another sea voyage brought them to Bombay (see p. 191).

The territorial divisions are those of the 1780s and 90s, when the Daniells were travelling.

1976 my husband and I were able to cover much of the Daniells' route, especially in the South. It is less easy to follow the old river route in the North, the railway having ousted the former river transport. Nevertheless Eric Newby, as his *Slowly down the Ganges* (1966) showed, managed to emulate the early travellers. The published arrangement of the aquatints is listed in Appendix I, so that anyone acquiring a print can identify the subject and relate it to the Daniells' work as a whole.

Each reproduction is accompanied by a note which frequently includes a quotation from the journal which William Daniell kept during part of the journey. Quotations for which no source is given are all taken from the small octavo booklets of comments which Thomas Daniell issued with each part of *Oriental Scenery*, but which are now almost impossible to obtain. These often reflect his own attitudes to the subjects he was depicting and also reveal the state of knowledge concerning Indian antiquities at that time. Quotations from the journals of other travellers are indicated by names and dates.

The spelling of Indian words and place-names has long been a vexed question. As long ago as 1847 Thomas de Quincey complained that the subject was 'at sixes and sevens, so that now most Hindoo words are in masquerade'. In the eighteenth century spelling was mainly phonetic. Now, since Independence, more correct spellings have been introduced for certain names, such as 'Tiruchchirappalli', for Trichinopoly, but these are still unfamiliar. In this book a middle course has been adopted. In the titles of the pictures the Daniells' own spelling has been preserved (with its own inconsistencies), but in the text the transliteration used in the *Imperial Gazetteer of India* (Oxford, 1931) has been followed, and the old well-known names, such as Trichinopoly, Benares and Cawnpore, have been kept. Where modern names are substantially different, this is indicated in the index.

For many years my husband and I have derived great delight from the Daniells, not only in following their travels but in collecting their drawings, oils and engravings. I would like to thank the many friends who over the years have shared our enthusiasm, especially our son and daughter, Giles Eyre, Maurice Shellim, Pauline Rohatgi, and Mary and Ronald Lightbown, and also Professor Walter Spink, who kindly advised me on the rock-cut temples of Western India. It is hoped that this book will tempt others to discover the Daniells and their work.

MILDRED ARCHER 1980

Note on the plates sections

In the captions, prints from the six series commonly known as *Oriental Scenery* are referred to by series number, an abbreviated version of the title under which that series was originally published, and the number of the print in that series. Series I–III are referred to as *Oriental Scenery*, the specially fine series IV as *Twenty-Four Landscapes*, series V as *Antiquities of India*, and series VI as *Hindoo Excavations in the Mountain of Ellora.*

In the reproductions, occasionally part of the sky is omitted; where a detail of a print is used the whole image is also included.

Information on the colour plates will be found in the captions to the corresponding black-and-white plates: II (24) for instance, refers to aquatint no. 24.

The Daniells

In 1784 a little-known artist, Thomas Daniell (1749–1840), decided to go to India with his young nephew, William (1769–1837). Although a brave decision it was not perhaps a surprising one. During the last quarter of the eighteenth century the power of the East India Company had greatly increased and the British were controlling large areas of the sub-continent. Although Bombay was still a small enclave confined to a group of marshy islands, Calcutta was the administrative centre of a great tract of land that extended up-country to Oudh. In the South, in spite of periodic confrontations with the rulers of Mysore, Madras dominated a considerable area and had good relations with the neighbouring rulers of the Carnatic and Tanjore. Many hazards and discomforts still accompanied life in India but there were now wide areas where an Englishman could travel freely and rely on hospitality from his countrymen. The Presidency cities of Calcutta and Madras had developed a way of life similar to that of an English provincial town such as Bath and they contained many wealthy residents who were happy to purchase pictures to furnish their large mansions.

By 1784 tales of the ease with which fortunes could be made in India were circulating in British artistic circles. Tilly Kettle had worked in Madras, Faizabad and Calcutta between 1769 and 1776; George Willison had been in Madras from 1774 to 1788 and had been well patronized by the Nawab of the Carnatic. Both artists had returned with considerable fortunes and had spoken well of the market that awaited a British artist there. In 1784 John Seton, George Farington, Charles Smith, John Zoffany and Thomas Hickey were all working in India and they too appeared to be prospering. Admittedly all were portrait painters. Of greater interest to Thomas Daniell, therefore, was William Hodges (1744–97), who, after accompanying Captain Cook on his second voyage to the Pacific in 1772–75, had visited India between 1780 and 1783. It is true that his movements there were somewhat hampered by political events and ill-health. While he was in Madras the Second Mysore War was in progress and it was unsafe for him to move far from the Presidency city. Similarly in Northern India he was unable to reach Delhi, which was in the control of the Marathas, but by joining up with a British political embassy he visited Gwalior and parts of Central India and moved on to Agra and Lucknow. In Bengal he had the good fortune to be patronized by Warren Hastings and by Augustus Cleveland, the District Officer of Bhagalpur, with whom he toured wild forested areas in Bihar. Hodges' experiences showed that it was perfectly feasible for a landscape artist to travel in India and find good patrons. He had returned to England in June 1784 with a large stock of drawings which he was planning to engrave. Thomas Daniell was undoubtedly encouraged by the experiences of these artists, especially Hodges. As regards the wealth of potential patrons in Calcutta there had recently been an example near his old home at Chertsey: Richard Barwell, a retired nabob, had come in 1781 to live on the Abbey House estate, which his father, a former Governor of Fort William, had purchased. It was rumoured that he had returned with a fortune of £400,000. If he was typical, then prospects were bright.

At the same time Daniell was aware of changing attitudes in Britain to landscape and architecture. Horizons were widening; a new approach to history was leading to a romantic awareness of the past. Scholars were beginning to explore other cultures and other periods. The essential qualities of 'beauty' were being questioned. Much had been written on the subject by theorists such as Edmund Burke, Richard Payne Knight and Uvedale Price. Fresh criteria were being applied which turned attention to the sensations and psychological influences that determined an aesthetic experience. New categories such as the 'sublime', the 'picturesque', and the 'exotic' were being valued in art and were constantly being defined and redefined. The colossal, all that was dark, melancholy or terrifying was linked with the sublime; romantic disorder, irregularity, intricacy and singular shapes were seen as 'picturesque' – a category fully expatiated upon and popularized by Dr Gilpin. Strange new architectural forms, tropical flora and fauna, 'native' manners and customs all conjured up the exotic. These qualities frequently intermingled in a single work. Such ideas were further strengthened by a new scientific approach to the world represented by the Royal Society. Nature, as Hodges had shown on Captain Cook's second voyage, could be carefully observed and accurately recorded so as to present a completely new vision of the world. This surely could be done for India also.

It was undoubtedly a combination of these various factors that prompted Thomas Daniell to apply to the East India Company for permission to go to India. At this time he, like many other British artists, was finding it difficult to earn a livelihood in England. He had become an artist the hard way. He came of humble origins: his father, John Sheppard Daniell, was lessee of the Swan Inn at Chertsey which was owned by a local family of mercers and drapers named Chapman. Thomas had started life by assisting his bricklayer brother but in 1763 he was apprenticed to a coach-builder, a Mr Maxwell, where he learnt the elementary skills of painting. In 1770, after completing his apprenticeship, he worked for several years for Charles Catton, coach-painter to George III. During this time, however, he must have felt an urge to become a professional artist for in 1772 he exhibited a flower painting at the Royal Academy. In 1773 he entered the Royal Academy Schools; between 1772 and 1784 he showed thirty pictures in Royal Academy exhibitions. It is clear that he had not yet decided what type of painting to concentrate on. He exhibited flower-pieces, a portrait, a dog-portrait and illustrations of literary subjects drawn from Spenser's *Faerie Queen*. In 1781 he secured a useful commission for six

View of the south colonnade front of the house, West Wycombe Park, by Thomas Daniell, 1781. (Private collection)

Thomas and William Daniell, sketched by John Downman in 1799, a few years after their return from India. The energetic William is wearing the uniform of the St Pancras Volunteers, one of the troops raised against the threat of Napoleon. (British Museum, London)

paintings of West Wycombe Park from its owner, the Rt Hon. Lord Le Despencer. During the next three years he showed landscapes painted in Somerset, Yorkshire and Oxfordshire which included natural phenomena such as Mother Shipton's Dropping Well near Knaresborough and Wookey Hole in Somerset. The views of West Wycombe were conventional classical landscapes, but the paintings of caves and rocks suggest that he was now developing a more romantic approach to landscape and was aware of changing attitudes.

At this time opportunities for landscape painters were few. During the last quarter of the eighteenth century patrons employed British artists chiefly for portraits, which showed the sitters either alone or with their families in their homes or gardens. For landscape paintings they still looked abroad and purchased from French, Italian or Dutch artists. As a result most British artists concentrated on portrait painting. Reynolds and Gainsborough dominated the scene but many other highly proficient painters were also practising. Competition was stiff and minor artists were often forced to lower their sights and become miniature painters or engravers. It was not surprising that Daniell was finding it difficult to establish himself. Moreover he had heavy family responsibilities. His brother, who had succeeded their father as landlord of the Swan, had died in 1779, leaving a widow who carried on the business but, with five children, was finding life hard. Thomas, probably in order to help her, took over the responsibility for his nephew William, who accompanied him to London and began to help him with his painting.

Late in 1784, therefore, in view of all these difficulties, Thomas Daniell sought permission to go to India as 'an engraver'. The form of his application is intriguing, for it is not clear how much experience he had had of this technique. There was, however, at the time a lively interest in the new process of aquatinting (see p. 14) which had been introduced into England by Paul Sandby only nine years earlier. Thomas Daniell, to judge by his later work, had almost certainly begun to experiment in this medium. It was a process which held out great possibilities for landscape artists through its similarity to the watercolour technique. It was well known that there was a great shortage of engravers in the Indian Presidency towns and Daniell may have thought that he could earn a modest income by this means in Calcutta while settling down to explore the market there. He may also have already conceived the idea of producing a series of engravings of Indian subjects. On the other hand, the form of his application may merely have been a prudent device for gaining permission to go to Calcutta. The East India Company knew well that the size of the British population in India who could afford to patronize artists was small. As we have seen, in 1784 at least five artists were already there. The Company did not want to find itself responsible for 'drop-outs' who needed to be supported or repatriated. For this reason it closely scrutinized all applications and reliable sureties had to be provided by every artist. John Smart, Ozias Humphry and Francis Wheatley had applied in September 1783 for permission to go to India: when granting it in July 1784 the Company specified that no more artists 'should be permitted to proceed to the East Indies this season'. Knowing this, Daniell may well have decided that he had more chance of being allowed to go if he described himself as an engraver.

A short time after submitting his own application he also sought permission to take with him, as an assistant, his nephew William, now aged fifteen. On 1 December 1784 his own application was approved by the Court of Directors and ten days later permission was given for William to accompany him. On 23 February 1785 Thomas Daniell gave the names of two artist friends, Robert Smirke and Edmund Hague, as securities. (Smirke was a painter of humorous and sentimental subjects and Hague was later referred to by Daniell as 'a painter of ceilings, friezes, chimney pieces etc. in the grotesque way with a good deal of taste'.) All was now ready for uncle and nephew to depart.

The voyage out; Calcutta April 1785 to August 1788

THE TWO DANIELLS set sail from Gravesend on 7 April 1785 on board the East Indiaman *Atlas*, bound for Canton. At this period the Company's most lucrative trade was with China and it was by no means easy to secure a direct passage to India. Many travellers were forced to go first to China and then find a country ship which would take them back to India. This was the course that the Daniells had to follow. They reached Whampoa on 23 August via Madeira, the Cape of Good Hope and the Straits of Sunda. It is not known how long they stayed in China, but they appear to have arrived in Calcutta early in 1786, after a journey back from China which would have taken about three months. They approached Calcutta across the Bay of Bengal and up the Hooghly River, delighting in the lush vegetation of the delta area (*nos. 1–3*).

Remaining loyal to his application, Thomas Daniell placed the following announcement in the *Calcutta Chronicle* of 17 July 1786: 'Mr Daniell proposes to publish twelve views of Calcutta at twelve gold Mohurs the set, from complete plates and finished watercolours. The subscription list is open till Jan. 1, 1787.' The advertisement was republished on 4 January 1787. The choice of subject was a wise decision, for there was clearly a ready market amongst the British population for engravings of the city. When the Daniells arrived Calcutta was thriving both politically and commercially and was rapidly expanding. After the battle of Buxar in 1764 military threats from the Mughals had ceased, and the city had begun to develop peacefully. By 1786 it had become a dignified place with fine buildings. A new Fort had been built on the river about a mile to the south, and the open space around it, which had originally been cleared to give firing space, now became the green Maidan where citizens took the air. The British residential area north of the Fort was rebuilt and improved, Esplanade Row and Chowringhi were laid out (*nos. 13, 10*), and fine Palladian houses, well adapted to the climate, began to spring up. Many citizens also built garden houses along the river, both north and south of the city, where they could escape from their work and the heat of their offices. During the ten years before the Daniells arrived many new public buildings had been completed – Writers' Buildings (*no. 5*), where the young members of the Company's Civil Service were housed, the New Court House

The chapter-head vignettes are taken from the title pages of *Oriental Scenery*. (India Office Library and Records, London)

(*no. 8*) at the west end of the Esplanade, and along this imposing street Government House, the Council House, the Accountant General's Office and the Supreme Court. St John's Church (*no. 15*) was still being built and was not consecrated until 1787. The docks as well as the ghats (*no. 9*), where the boats disembarked their passengers, were gradually being improved. Calcutta was indeed becoming the 'City of Palaces'. The stucco, re-whitewashed after every rainy season, shone in the brilliant sunlight, set off by green lawns and luxuriant flowering trees. As Thomas Daniell himself was later to write of the city, 'The splendour of British arms produced sudden change in its aspects; the bamboo roof suddenly vanished, the marble column took the place of brick walls; princely mansions were erected by private individuals.' When Count Grandpré visited Calcutta in 1789 he described it as 'not only the handsomest town in Asia but one of the finest in the world'. The citizens of Calcutta were taking a pride in its development and would clearly appreciate views of the new buildings.

The production of the aquatints, however, proceeded slowly. The Daniells in order to support themselves had to accept miscellaneous routine work such as the repair or cleaning of oil paintings for both private individuals and the East India Company. In September 1787 they submitted a bill for 1,500 sicca rupees for cleaning and rehanging pictures which had been moved from the Old Court House to the Council Room. Three engravings were nevertheless produced in 1786, four in 1787 and five in 1788 (*nos. 4–15*). On 10 May 1787 the *Calcutta Chronicle* had announced that 'Mr Daniell has completed six of the views and will deliver impressions as soon as possible. Non subscribers 18 Gold Mohurs.' The *Calcutta Gazette* of the same date announced, 'Mr Daniell having completed six of his views hopes to deliver prints in the course of the next month. The remainder will be delivered as finished. He begs subscribers to forward the amount of their subscription.'

Of all engraving techniques, aquatint is one of the most difficult and complex, demanding great experience and judgment. The process was succinctly described by Thomas Sutton in his pioneer book on the Daniells:

> A highly polished copper-plate is coated with wax, which is then held in the smoke of a taper until the surface, having melted gently, is an even golden brown. Upon this the original subject is then drawn or traced in reverse, the pencil lines showing clearly against the now hardened wax. The highest lights are now 'stopped out' with an acid-resisting substance and the plate placed in a box containing thousands of tiny particles of powdered resin. Upon the turning of a handle, a current of air is created, causing the particles to rise and then settle like dust upon the waxed surface of the plate. This is now placed in a bath of acid, which bites into the plate where the dust has disturbed, however slightly, the wax. The plate is then removed, thoroughly rinsed, and the parts judged to have been sufficiently bitten are 'stopped out'. The process is repeated, the bitings become successively deeper, until the strongest darks are reached. The wax is then removed and the copper-plate is seen to be pitted everywhere by minute holes, except where 'stopping out' has been employed. The resultant print consists not of lines of varying depth or thickness, as in an etching or a copper-plate engraving, but of tones.

The effect is similar to the foundation washes of sepia and grey, or 'dead colouring', which were used in watercolours of the late eighteenth century. By

Old Court House Street, Calcutta (detail of *Views of Calcutta*, 12, 1788). Before a backdrop of dignified European houses, a covered bullock-cart is turning; beyond it a sedan chair waits; on the left, a European is carried in a palanquin; in the foreground, a soldier strolls with an Indian woman. A horse is stabled at the far right.

the time the print had been hand-coloured the aquatint was an almost exact replica of the watercolour original (compare p. 96 and colour plate XI).

In their Calcutta days, however, Thomas Daniell was not yet highly skilled in aquatinting, and William was only learning the technique. They had to use local Indian craftsmen to help them pull off the prints and 'stain' (i.e. colour) them. Thomas's friend, William Baillie, was later to write on 23 November 1793, 'All Daniell's Views were stained principally by natives.' Work of this type was new to them also and Thomas Daniell was clearly disappointed with the result. Writing to Ozias Humphry on 7 November 1788, he said,

> The Lord be praised, at length I have completed my twelve views of Calcutta. The fatigue I have experienced in this undertaking has almost worn me out. . . . It will appear a very poor performance in your land, I fear. You must look upon it as a *Bengalee* work. You know I was obliged to stand Painter,

Engraver, Coppersmith, Printer and Printer's Devil myself. It was a *devilish* undertaking but I was determined to see it through at all events.

Though the early *Views of Calcutta* include etched lines and are less softly watercolour-like than the aquatints the Daniells were to make after their return to England, they were nevertheless highly popular. No other engravings of the city existed apart from the outdated early prints by Elisha Kirkall and Gerard Vandergucht published in 1735 and 1736, based on the oils made in England by George Lambert and Samuel Scott, and a print by Jan van Ryne published in 1754. All of them were merely general views showing the city from across the river. Although William Hodges had made drawings, it was not until 1794 that he published an engraving of Fort William. The Daniells' views gave careful and accurate depictions of the main public buildings, especially those of interest to Company servants, and in the foregrounds they showed in lively detail novel forms of transport and the varied social life of the city. The diarist William Hickey at once purchased a set: 'As I was always as great an encourager of merits as my humble means would allow, I not only subscribed myself but procured other names.' He was typical of many Calcutta residents and the prints sold well.

Detail of a plan of Calcutta by M. W. Wollaston, 1825. Since the Daniells had left a few buildings had been demolished, and a new Government House had been built (J), but the city was substantially the same. A Tank Square, B Writers' Buildings, C Old Fort, D Clive Street, E Old Court House Street and site of Old Court House, F St John's, G,G Esplanade Row, H New Court House and site of Council House, J Government House, K Maidan and New Fort William, L Chowringhi, M to Garden Reach and Kidderpore, N Govinda Ram Mitter's Pagoda, in Chitpore Road (running north-south). (India Office Library and Records, London)

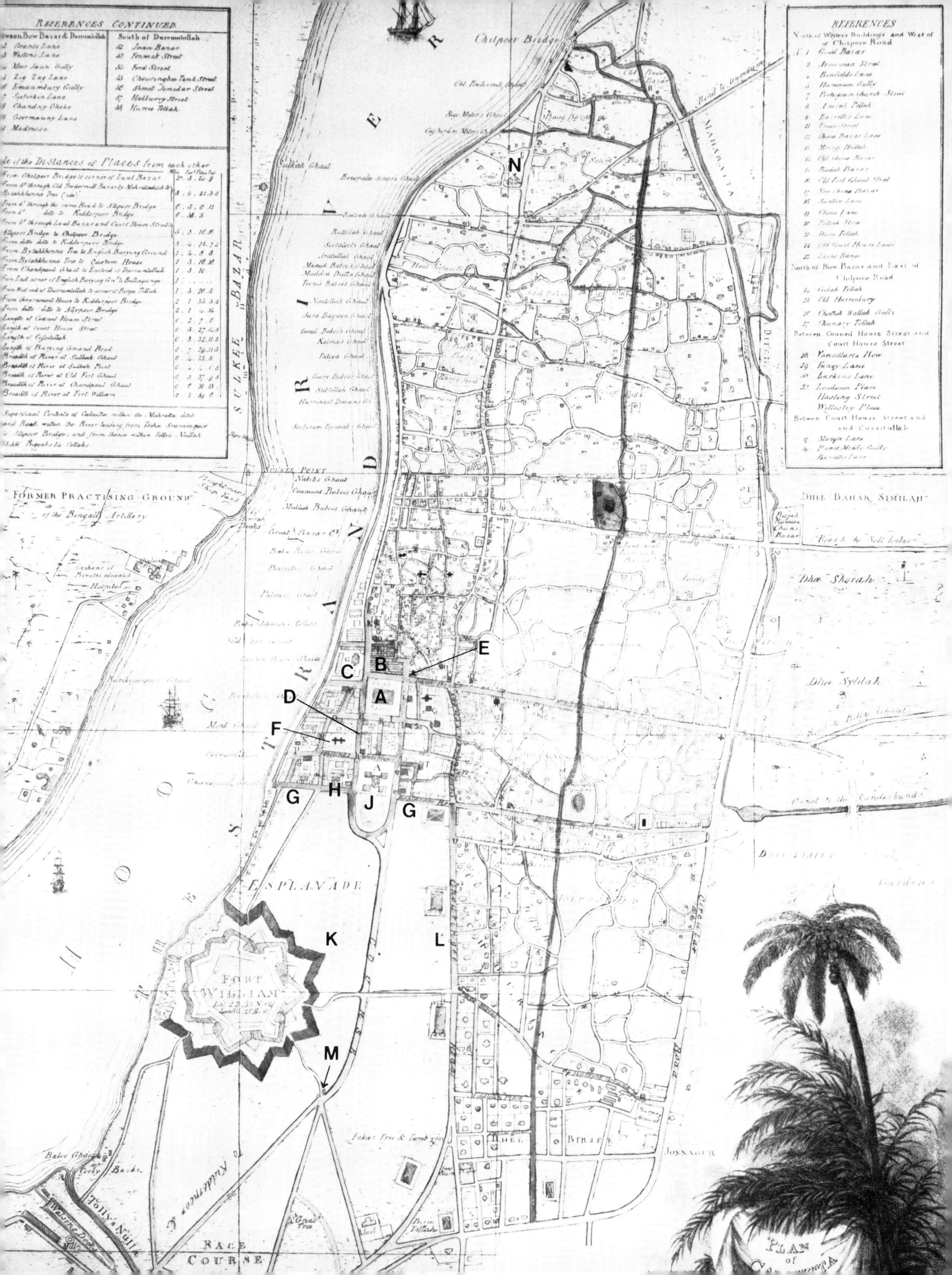

REFERENCES CONTINUED.
South of Durrumtollah
52 Jaun Bazar
53 Fenwick Street
54 Ford Street
55 Chowringhee Tank Street
56 Ahmet Jemidar Street
57 Halburry Street
58 Hurree Tollah
REFERENCES
North of Writers Buildings and West of Chitpore Road
No 1 Great Bazar
North of Bow Bazar and East of Chitpore Road
Between Council House Street and Court House Street
Between Court House Street and Cossitollah
Chitpore Bridge
Road to Dumdum
MAHARATTA
DITCH
RIVER
HOOGLY
SULKEE BAZAR
FORMER PRACTISING GROUND of the Bengall Artillery
Orphans & Privates Hospital
DHEE BAHAR SIMILAH
Road to the Salt lakes
Dhee Shorah
Dhee Syldah
Canal to the Sunderbunds
ESPLANADE
FORT WILLIAM
RACE COURSE
Tolly's Nullah
Circular Road
JONNAGUR
PLAN of
A
B
C
D
E
F
G
H
J
K
L
M
N

1

2

1 'Fowl Island, Bay of Bengal' (*A Picturesque Voyage to India*, 46)
1786(?). Thomas and William Daniell arrived in India from England via China, travelling back from Canton to Calcutta by a 'country ship' which was registered in an Indian port and engaged in trade in Eastern waters. Before reaching India it took on water at Fowl Island off the coast of Arakan. The ship shown is most probably that in which the Daniells were sailing.

2 'Near Cucrahattee, on the River Hoogly' (*A Picturesque Voyage to India*, 48)
1786(?). 'This view is taken from a spot near the Hoogly, embellished by nature with all the exuberance of vegetation peculiar to Bengal . . . but the eye is perpetually offended by pieces of stagnant water, which generate impure air and myriads of insects . . . Of these the most formidable are the musquitoes, which are merely gnats of a gigantic size. It is curious to observe how completely sensation is subdued by custom and the operation of superstitious prejudice. The poor Hindoo, anxious to ensure his performance of those daily ablutions which constitute an essential part of worship, erects his hut on the margin of these polluted streams, and felicitates himself on the circumstance that exposes him to probable danger and inevitable inconvenience.'

Once their ship entered the Hooghly delta, many of the British thought all their perils were over. They delighted in the rural beauty of villages such as Kukrahati on the river banks. But for some, dangers of a different sort had just begun. Myriads of malarial mosquitoes assaulted the passengers, while the heat caused some of the new arrivals to succumb before they even reached Calcutta. In the hot weather of 1782 Bob Potts' beautiful mistress, Emily Warren, according to the diarist William Hickey, suddenly collapsed and died after drinking glasses of cold water and milk. A memorial to her was later erected by her lover in the jungle on Sagar Island, a grisly welcome to newcomers.

3 'Near Gangwaugh Colly, on the River Hoogly' (*A Picturesque Voyage to India*, 47)
1786(?). 'This view is bounded by impenetrable forests; trees of gigantic growth rise among the underwood which overhangs the banks of the Hoogly, and forms a safe covert [for] the most fierce and formidable animals. The wild hog and buffalo are natives of this jungle, venomous snakes are nurtured in its luxurious verdure; and tygers, issuing from these delicious shades, are often bold enough to leap on the boats that ply near the coast: yet the deer, and other animals of the gentlest nature, are still found in the vicinity of their ferocious foes.'

The Sundarbans, the jungly area at the mouth of the Hooghly, was famous for its tigers, which were often to be seen swimming across the many channels of the river. When ships anchored to wait for the tide, British passengers, excited to be near land again, would sometimes disembark at places like this village of Geonkhali, to picnic or shoot game. While the Daniells were in India, the British public was horrified by the news that the only son of Sir Hector Munro, while picknicking on Sagar Island, had been suddenly carried off by a tiger. A member of the party related how 'In a moment his head was in the beast's mouth and it rushed into the jungle with him, with as much ease as I could lift a kitten.'

4

5

4 'The Old Fort, the Playhouse, Holwell's Monument' (*Views of Calcutta*, 1, 1786)
We are looking north along Clive Street, past the eastern wall of Old Fort William, on the left (*no.* 9). On the right is the memorial to the tragedy of the Black Hole which had taken place inside the Fort in 1756. When Siraj-ud-Daula, Nawab of Bengal, attacked Calcutta in June that year, a number of the British who had not fled surrendered and were locked for the night in a stifling cell. Next morning only a few – perhaps a third – emerged alive. The memorial was erected by one of the survivors, John Zephaniah Holwell (see *no.* 95). In the centre background can be seen the Theatre built by public subscription in 1775. On the extreme right is part of Writers' Buildings (*no.* 5).

5 'The Old Court House and Writers' Buildings' (*Views of Calcutta*, 2, 1786)
This view is taken at right angles to that in *no.* 4, looking back towards the Old Fort and Monument. On the north side of Tank Square, facing the Tank (*no.* 6), was the Old Court House, built before the siege of 1756 and later enlarged. It was a handsome two-storeyed building with an open arcaded verandah. Ionic colums and a balustrade topped with urns. It was pulled down in 1792 and St Andrew's Church stands on the site. Between it and the Old Fort (visible in the distance) stood Writers' Buildings. East India Company servants when they first arrived were known as 'Writers'. They were usually unmarried and the problem of housing them for their first years was solved in 1780 by this long range of identical suites built by the Company's Engineer, Thomas Lyon. Sir Charles d'Oyly commented, in *Tom Raw, the Griffin* (1828),

> There to the northward, in one even line
> The Writers' Buildings stand – nineteen in number,
> Where young Civilians prosper or decline,
> As study spurs them, or o'er books they slumber.

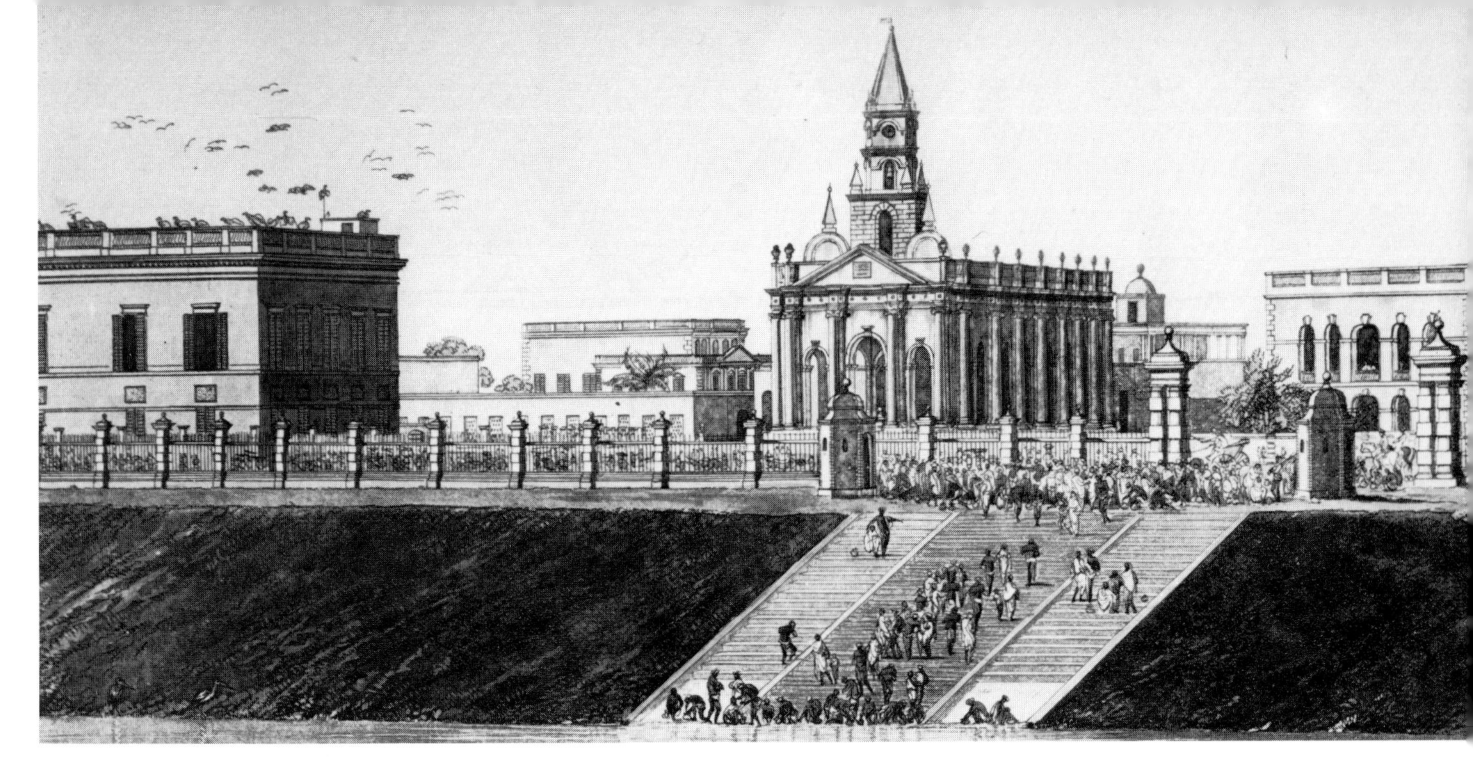

6

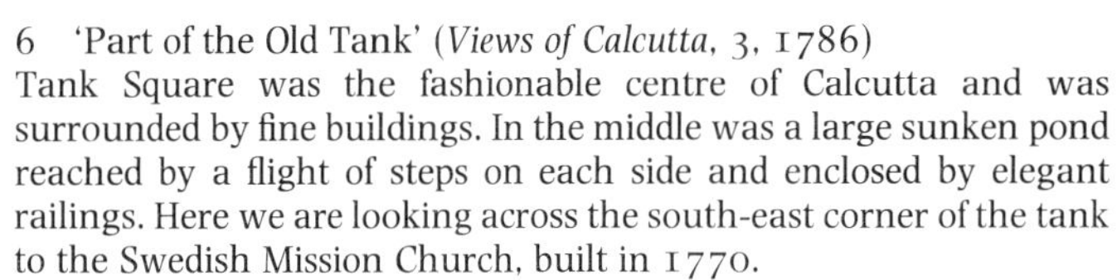

6 'Part of the Old Tank' (*Views of Calcutta*, 3, 1786)
Tank Square was the fashionable centre of Calcutta and was surrounded by fine buildings. In the middle was a large sunken pond reached by a flight of steps on each side and enclosed by elegant railings. Here we are looking across the south-east corner of the tank to the Swedish Mission Church, built in 1770.

7

7 'Gentoo Pagoda and House' (*Views of Calcutta*, 4, 1787)
The Chitpore Bazaar lay about 4 miles (*c.* 7 km) to the north of Calcutta. Unlike Madras, where the 'Black Town' was separated from the British city, the Indian bazaars and houses of Calcutta merged on the outskirts. Various wealthy Indians had lived at Chitpore, including Nawab Muhammad Reza Khan, and a wealthy Hindu ('Gentoo') landlord, Govinda Ram Mitter. The latter had built a temple, known as the Black Pagoda, in about 1730 and Thomas Daniell made two views of it, this and *no.* 97. Small though it was, he was clearly interested in its architecture for he had as yet seen no Hindu temple of any significance.

8

8 'The New Court House and Chandpam Ghaut' (*Views of Calcutta*, 5, 1787)
The New Court House, on the site of the present High Court, stood at the western end of Esplanade Row (*no. 13*), a fine thoroughfare which ran at right angles to the river facing the open green Maidan around the new Fort William. Finished in 1784, it replaced the Old Court House (*no. 5*) which, after the arrival of the Judges of the Supreme Court in 1775, had proved too small. It was a dignified building with Ionic columns lining a long open verandah which extended the whole length of the first floor.

The varied social life of Calcutta is brilliantly caught in this print – a dandy chats to an elegant lady in a sedan chair, bearers wait beside their master's palanquin, and a religious procession, bearing flags on long poles and a model 'peacock boat', hurries down to the river at Chandpal Ghat.

9

10

9 'The Old Fort Ghaut' (*Views of Calcutta*, 6, 1787)
The Old Fort Ghat adjoined the Old Fort (compare the bastion in *no. 4*). Thomas Twining described the scene when he arrived in 1792: 'I quitted the boat at a spacious sloping ghaut or landing-place, close to the north-west angle of the old fort. The lower part of the slope went some way into the water, and was crowded with natives, men and women, bathing with their clothes, or rather *cloths* on, and which they dexterously contrived to change under water, without embarrassment to themselves or the bystanders.'

The Old Fort had now been replaced for military purposes by the New Fort and was 'appropriated to the reception of the goods of the Company, and the merchandise of the custom-house, the direction of which was within its walls. Upon the custom-house wharf, extending from one end to the other, I saw immense piles of goods of various sorts, imports and exports.'

10 'The New Buildings at Chouringhee' (*Views of Calcutta*, 7, 1787)
Fine houses had begun to spring up in Chowringhi along the eastern side of the Maidan, facing the New Fort. Each stood in its own separate plot of land and was built according to the owner's taste and convenience. Most were in a Palladian style with pillared verandahs and balustraded roofs. This street was gradually to develop into Calcutta's most dignified thoroughfare, but in the Daniells' time it is clear that the area had been newly laid out. Various forms of transport are shown – pack bullocks, camels, an English carriage and Indian vehicles drawn by bullocks. The one with a domed canopy was known as a *rath*. The adjutant birds wading in the pond were the great scavengers of early Calcutta.

Chowringhi today is the main tourist and shopping centre of Calcutta. The Grand Hotel and the Ritz Continental Hotel are situated there, as well as the Indian Museum and the Headquarters of the Geological Survey.

11

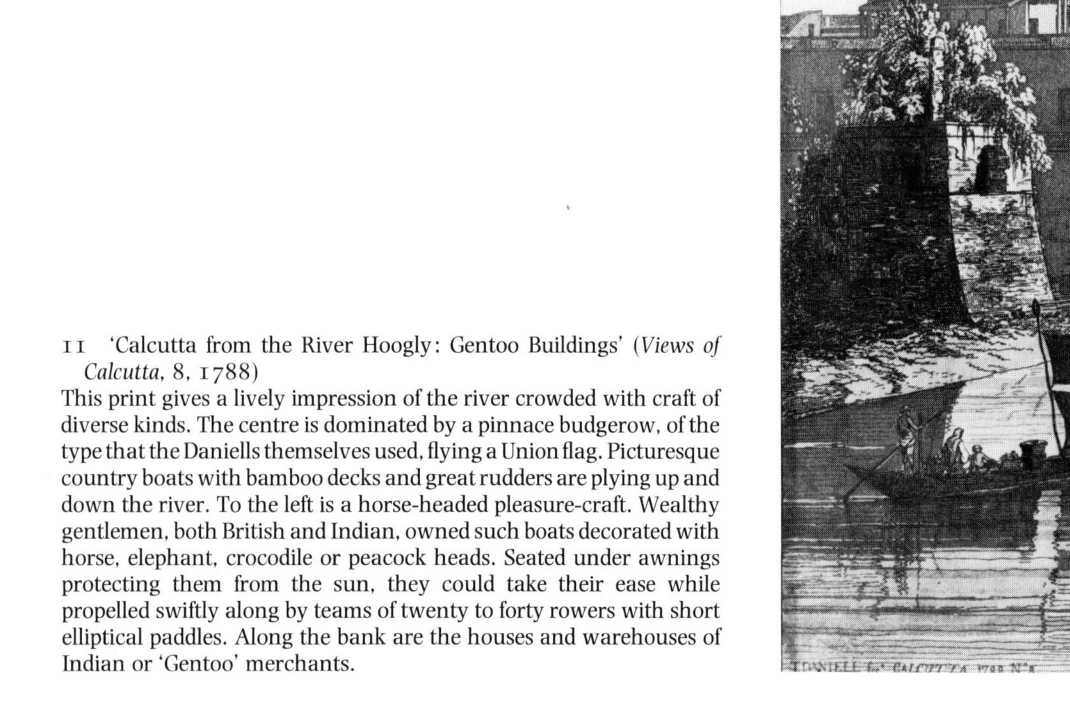

11 'Calcutta from the River Hoogly: Gentoo Buildings' (*Views of Calcutta*, 8, 1788)

This print gives a lively impression of the river crowded with craft of diverse kinds. The centre is dominated by a pinnace budgerow, of the type that the Daniells themselves used, flying a Union flag. Picturesque country boats with bamboo decks and great rudders are plying up and down the river. To the left is a horse-headed pleasure-craft. Wealthy gentlemen, both British and Indian, owned such boats decorated with horse, elephant, crocodile or peacock heads. Seated under awnings protecting them from the sun, they could take their ease while propelled swiftly along by teams of twenty to forty rowers with short elliptical paddles. Along the bank are the houses and warehouses of Indian or 'Gentoo' merchants.

12 'Old Court House Street looking South' (*Views of Calcutta*, 9, 1778
Old Court House Street ran north-south from the Old Court House (*no.* 5) in Tank Square along the eastern side of Government House to the Maidan. Its comfortable mansions of many different designs are set in compounds on either side of the road. The street is busy with varying forms of Indian and British transport – an elephant, a canopied bullock carriage, sedan chairs, palanquins and carriages. People of many types, including an ascetic, mingle in the road.

13

13 'Esplanade Row and the Council House' (*Views of Calcutta*, 10, 1788)

East of the New Court House in Esplanade Row (see *no. 8*) was the Accountant General's Office – in the centre, here – and next to it the Council House of 1764 with two projecting wings. The latter was pulled down in 1800. Between these two buildings is the spire of St John's Church, consecrated in 1787 (*no. 15*). In the foreground is the grassy Maidan, then as now the green lung of Calcutta. Various servants can be seen on the Maidan, including a syce leading a horse and a doriya or dog-boy exercising his master's pets. Originally the Maidan had been a rough area kept free of scrub to provide an open firing space from the Fort, but with the completion of the New Fort to the south in 1773 it became a fine grassy stretch where Calcutta inhabitants could 'eat the air'. The Daniells included another view of the area in *Oriental Scenery* (*no. 94*).

14

14 'Old Government House' (*Views of Calcutta*, 11, 1788)

Government House was situated in Esplanade Row facing the Maidan. It had been built in 1767 next to the Council House of 1764, which is seen on the far right of the previous print. It was an elegant Palladian building similar in style to the Old Court House (*no. 5*), with Ionic columns on the first floor level and a roof-balustrade with urns. In the foreground of this view a wealthy Indian visitor in his palanquin, surrounded by retainers and followed by elephants, is about to enter the right-hand gate; in the centre are guards and kettle-drummers on camel-back.

T.DANIELL fec. Calcutta 1788 W 12

15 'St John's Church' (*Views of Calcutta*, 12, 1788)
St John's, begun in 1784, was not completed until 1787, after the Daniells' arrival. Its designer was James Agg, a young Lieutenant of the Bengal Engineers. He adopted the basic model of St Martin's-in-the-Fields, London, simplifying it to suit local conditions. In order to avoid a drive across the old consecrated burial ground, which can be seen in the distance, the portico was placed at the east end, behind the altar. (The arrangement was changed in 1811.) Here worshippers are arriving in palanquins and carriages of various types, which waited for their owners until the service was over.

16

16 'Old Fort Gaut, Calcutta' (*A Picturesque Voyage to India*, 50)
Another view of the scene shown in *no. 9*.

17 'View of Calcutta from the Garden Reach' (*A Picturesque Voyage to India*, 49)
Garden Reach lay south of the city, providing a delightful welcome to the newcomer as he sailed up the river past the 'garden houses' and a last glimpse as he departed. William Hickey, when he arrived in 1777, was 'greatly pleased by a rich and magnificent view of a number of splendid houses, the residences of gentlemen of the highest rank in the Company's service who, with their families, usually left Calcutta in the hot season to enjoy the cooler and more refreshing air of these pleasant situations. . . . The verdure throughout on every side was beautiful beyond imagination, the whole of the landscape being more luxuriant than I had any expectation of seeing in the burning climate of Bengal.'

At the same time there was a splendid view of the distant city, with the main official buildings, including Government House, silhouetted on the skyline. The Daniells had drawn this scene during their stay in Calcutta. By 1810, however, when they were preparing *A Picturesque Voyage to India*, they knew that their original drawing was out of date, for Marquis Wellesley had built a new and grander Government House after they had left. The artists therefore modified their drawing and incorporated the new building, perhaps using James Moffat's aquatint of it which had been published in 1805.

17

Up the country August 1788 to April 1789

WITH THE VIEWS OF CALCUTTA completed and ready money in hand, Thomas Daniell began to plan a tour up-country. This had certainly been in his mind from the start. His aim was to collect a large body of drawings which could be put to varied use at a later date for the working up of finished watercolours, oils and engravings. During the busy years in Calcutta he had been collecting information about places he would like to visit. While tied to the Presidency town he had had no opportunity to explore 'Indian India'. The city was a new foundation: apart from a few minor temples and mosques he had been unable to see any great Indian monuments or even any truly Indian town. Moreover the surrounding countryside of the Hooghly delta was flat and undistinguished and he could form no idea of the varied scenery of India.

There is no doubt that the arrival in Calcutta between 1786 and 1788 of William Hodges' *Select Views* had given Thomas Daniell a clear idea of the use to which drawings could be put. It also gave him suggestions for places to visit. A journey up-country by the well-known river route to Cawnpore and then on to Delhi and Agra was an obvious choice. Although Thomas had a kind and generous nature he was obviously irked by the publication of the *Select Views*. Hodges had to some degree forestalled him and was a rival. The young William was indignant and highly critical of Hodges' work. He clearly considered his uncle a far better draughtsman. Nevertheless Hodges had set a standard as a pioneering recorder of India, and his views became a guide in general terms to the route that they should follow. The Daniells decided to outdo him, to see for themselves the tombs, mosques, temples and picturesque scenes that he had depicted and to make a more impressive and more accurate record of those same places (compare p. 99 and *nos.* 69, 73).

They also had plans to be far more adventurous. During their stay in Calcutta, they had come to know some of the scholarly and enterprising inhabitants of Bengal and had learnt much from them about places of interest. Charles Wilkins, the great Sanskritist, who had been living in Benares translating Sanskrit texts, was in Calcutta when they first arrived. From him the Daniells must have learnt much about Hindu monuments in Benares and about the importance of other sacred cities such as Mathura, Brindaban,

Ayodhya and Hardwar. Dr William Hunter, a surgeon in Bengal, was a keen antiquarian, and in 1785 had published an account of the caves of Western India. Major William Palmer was another friend. In 1786 he had returned to Calcutta from Lucknow and was commanding the 7th Battalion of Sepoys before going in 1787 as Resident to the Court of Sindhia, the Maratha chief in Delhi. He gave the Daniells much advice and offered to show them the sights of Delhi and Agra. The Frenchman Colonel Claud Martin, who was in the service of the Nawab of Oudh at Lucknow, visited Calcutta from time to time. He was a generous patron of the arts and promised to give the Daniells hospitality if they visited Lucknow. Several fellow artists based on Calcutta had already made forays up-country. John Zoffany, Charles Smith, Ozias Humphry and Francesco Renaldi could all have been helpful, while Sir William Jones, who had arrived in Calcutta in 1783, was a stimulating source of information on antiquities. He had been prominent in the formation in 1784 of the Asiatic Society of Bengal, of which Thomas Daniell became a member. Jones's letters show that he kept in touch with Thomas and from time to time discussed illustrations for the Society's journal, *Asiatic Researches.*

Another important influence on the Daniells' projected tour was Samuel Davis, Assistant District Officer of Bhagalpur. He too paid visits to Calcutta and became a great friend of the artists. He was a competent amateur painter and during 1783 had accompanied Turner's embassy to Tibet. Political problems had prevented him from proceeding beyond Bhutan, but while Turner was away he had filled the time by making numerous drawings of the snowy ranges, the great hills and the villages with their wooden houses. There is little doubt that he encouraged the Daniells to include a visit to the foothills of the Himalayas so that they could gain at least a taste of the grand mountain scenery and a glimpse of the snows, which were as yet almost unknown.

In the light of all this advice from friends and acquaintances the Daniells planned their first tour. Since at this time no hotels or official rest-houses existed in India, it was essential to plot a route which would give them a chance to stay with friends, who would give them hospitality and also assist with arrangements for the next stage of the journey. Considerations such as these undoubtedly helped to determine the route, but at the same time it was wise to be flexible and seize any alternative opportunity for exploring the countryside. If, for example, they encountered a military contingent about to move into a relatively unknown or unsettled area, then they should join up with it.

Above all it was essential to remember the vagaries of the climate. The cold weather was the ideal time for sight-seeing on the plains, while the hottest months of the year, April and May, would be best spent in the hills. The monsoon rains in July and August made it impossible to travel or sketch, so it would be wise to stay with friends then and use the time to complete drawings and work up oils.

A tour of this type was a formidable undertaking. The Daniells had no great reserves of money and therefore had to travel economically. They had no official backing and could only afford a few servants. Not for them the great tour with a vast train of servants which was organized for important British officials. They took with them two attendants – Charles and Johnny Diaz, both of whom were probably Eurasians of mixed Indian and Portuguese blood. They also had a *sircar* (broker and house steward), a *kitmatgar* (table servant), a *chaukidar* (watchman) and two *kalassis* (tent pitchers). For the journey up-country it was

The palace-fort of Tashichodzong at Thimpu, Bhutan; watercolour by Samuel Davis, 1783. (India Office Library and Records, London)

necessary to hire a crew of *dandies* and a pinnace budgerow, on which they could live and sleep. The quarters were cramped – a living room measuring about 24 by 18 feet (7 by 5·5 metres), a smaller bedroom and a narrow vestibule. It was also necessary to hire an unwieldy *patella* or baggage boat. A journey by water was full of hazards, for the Ganges was a vast and dangerous river, subject to sudden storms. Without skilled handling the wind, the fast currents, rocks, sandbanks and falling cliffs could wreck a boat. Even on leaving Calcutta, the river bore had to be avoided. And unless great tact was exercised throughout the expedition the crew or servants might desert and disappear overnight.

A journey overland also had its own problems. Although James Rennell had begun to publish his fine maps of Bengal and Upper India in 1780, it was frequently necessary to rely on local villagers as guides. A large part of Bengal and Bihar was now administered by the British and a British force was stationed in Oudh, but hostile Marathas were in control of Delhi and Central India. Further north the Punjab Hills were ruled by local rajas who from time to time waged war on each other. Dacoity or banditry was common everywhere and there could well be danger for a small party of Englishmen. It was wise to be self-sufficient, since European goods were not available outside the major towns. For

A pinnace budgerow with Europeans seated on deck below an awning, almost certainly an illustration of the Daniells' own boat, from their aquatint of Ramnagar (*no. 23*).

the Daniells a large supply of artists' materials was essential – paper, pencils, brushes, paints, canvases and stretchers – for none could be procured locally during the journey. It was also necessary to live off the country. William had a gun and had grand ideas of shooting for the pot, but his diary shows that he had little success and their diet must often have been monotonous.

Nevertheless generous help was at times available. East India Company servants, both civil and military, were posted to many of the towns through which the Daniells planned to pass. These officers frequently spent lonely lives in isolated stations and were delighted to be hospitable. New faces, especially if the visitors were interesting characters, were heartily welcomed and provided with shelter, food and advice. When they left, the visitors were often given a stock of food to help them on the next leg of their journey.

Above all the Daniells were themselves determined characters. During their two-and-a-half years in Calcutta they had become used to the ways of the country. They must have acquired sufficient of the language to manage the servants. Thomas, in particular, had enormous strength of character and appears to have been rarely ruffled. William was young and adaptable, full of enthusiasm and energy. Both men had strong constitutions. In the years that followed they appear to have had only a few days' indisposition. The two artists in fact were admirably fitted to undertake a long tour 'up the country'.

On 29 August 1788, when the rains were almost ending, Thomas and William Daniell set off from their garden house at Kidderpore. They were not to return to Calcutta until late 1791 – more than three years later. During this time a large part of their travels is documented by a boyish and somewhat flat diary which William kept from the day they left until 19 May 1789. There then follows a break until 8 July, when the diary begins again and continues until 30 January 1790. Their movements during the intervening periods can be largely reconstructed from the dates and titles which they carefully inscribed on the backs of their pencil and watercolour drawings (now housed in a number of collections). At times William's spelling of place-names is confusing and in the published transcript of the diary words have sometimes been misread from the original manuscript. With the help of a modern map, however, the places they visited can almost all be identified. The Daniells took with them a perambulator (a wooden wheel with a mile-counter, pushed along the ground) and in the diary distances are frequently mentioned, thus helping to locate villages and small towns.

The Daniells left Calcutta itself on 3 September after loading up and waiting for the dangerous river bore to sweep past. The first stage of their journey, as far as Cawnpore, followed the route which, until the coming of the railways in the nineteenth century, was the most usual and comfortable method of travelling up-country. They sailed along the Hooghly, a branch of the Ganges delta, passing the European settlements of Chinsurah, Hooghly and Bandell (*no. 18*). The first month was spent sailing through the green low-lying countryside of Bengal. On 3 October they arrived at Murshidabad, the former capital of the Nawab of Bengal. On the 8th they reached the main stream of the River Ganges and the countryside began to change dramatically. On their left were the Rajmahal Hills covered in thick jungle where tigers, rhinoceros and wild elephants lurked. When they reached the town of Rajmahal itself they found the banks strewn with picturesque ruins. For a time the Mughal capital of Bengal and Bihar had been located here and the provincial governors had built numerous palaces and tombs in the area (*no. 19, I*). Many of these were now collapsing into the river and proving a hazard for boats. The Daniells made a point of visiting a caravanserai that Hodges had drawn and engraved. Three days later, guided by a hill-man, they set off to visit a waterfall – Moti Jharna, the Fall of Pearls – on the eastern side of the hills which they could see from the boat. Waterfalls, with their hint of the sublime, were to prove a constant attraction for the artists. On the way William was thrilled to see the footprint of a rhinoceros. As they sailed upstream, the countryside, vivid green after the rains, continued to be attractive. The promontory of Sakrigali (*no. 20*), where there was a pass into the hills, appeared highly picturesque. Soon they saw the Colgong Hills and negotiated the dangerous rocks where the current flowed like a mill-race. It was here that the boat of Warren Hastings' wife, Marian, had once been almost swamped and Hodges had recorded the incident in a dramatic oil. Nearby was the hill of Pathargatha with its temples and a holy cave.

At Bhagalpur, where their friend Samuel Davis was posted, palanquins were waiting to take them to his house and they spent the day of 18 October with him. It is most probable that here they discussed their future plans and were urged by him to try and reach the Himalayan foothills. Three days later they visited the hot springs of Sitakund and Pir Pahar, a hill topped by a large

Mughal house. On returning to the river they found to their dismay that the masts of the pinnace had broken during their absence. However, repairs were soon made and they continued along the great broad river, past the carved rocks of Sultanganj to Monghyr, with its fort. Here they visited Major Skelly and took along to show him two volumes of prints after Claude Lorraine, mezzotints by Richard Earlom made in 1777. They may have discussed with him the aquatints that they themselves were planning to produce, perhaps using Claude as a model. From Monghyr they continued to Patna with its long bazaar stretching along the river bank (*no. 21*). The local Nawab lent them a house by the river in which to stay. They visited the Civil Station of Bankipore, west of Patna, where William drew the beehive-shaped granary built by the engineer Colonel Garstin in 1786, on the orders of Warren Hastings, as protection against famine. (It was used for this purpose again almost two hundred years later, during 1966–67.) On 13 November they reached Maner, where they sketched the tomb of Makhdam Shah Daulat (*no. 22*) which Hodges had also drawn and greatly admired.

After negotiating the dangerous currents where the River Son flowed into the Ganges, the Daniells travelled on past Chapra to Buxar. Here the British in 1764 had defeated the Mughal Emperor and the Nawab of Oudh. On 25 November they reached Ghazipur where the East India Company had its opium factory. Once again they were guided by Hodges' *Select Views* to a number of picturesque buildings, including the palace, high up on the river bank, with its pleasure-pavilion, the Chalis Satun or Forty-Pillared Hall. William was interested to see that some boys were playing there with tops and spinning them exactly as in England. They also visited the Garden of Faiz Ali Khan, where fine tombs stood amongst the trees. Many years later Thomas was to make an attractive oil painting of this site. Here they were befriended by John Lloyd, the Commercial Resident, who laid on a nautch or display of dancing for them and the local gentry.

It was now December and it would seem that the Daniells were feeling slightly apprehensive lest they should fail to complete the first part of their tour before the weather became too hot. They had also heard, it appears, that a party of British officers at Fatehgarh were planning to visit Agra and Delhi. They decided therefore not to stop at Benares, where there would be so much to draw, but to sail past, completing only views of the city from the river (*no. 23*). At Chunar they fitted up the smallest baggage boat so as 'to get up quick to Cawnpore'. The first half of the month was spent sailing to Allahabad, passing park-like scenery with great trees, the river-banks sprinkled with numerous small temples and fragments of sculpture. At Allahabad, as at Benares, they only made views from the river (*no. 24, II*), hurrying on past Kara (*nos. 25, 26, III*) and Dalmau to Cawnpore, where they arrived in the last week of 1788.

Here the boats were paid off and the Daniells travelled overland to Fatehgarh where they joined the party of British officers. They had now left the Company's territory and were entering a less settled area dominated by the warlike Marathas. It was advisable to travel in a large body with the protection of an armed force. The party consisted of General Carnac, Colonel Briscoe, Major Lucius Smith, Captain Jonathan Wood and 'Melville, Bayley, Bushby and Clarkson', with their servants, two companies of sepoys, and a small body of horse, as well as elephants, camels, horses and bullocks. It was still the cold weather and William notes that they would set off at 5 a.m. and breakfast at

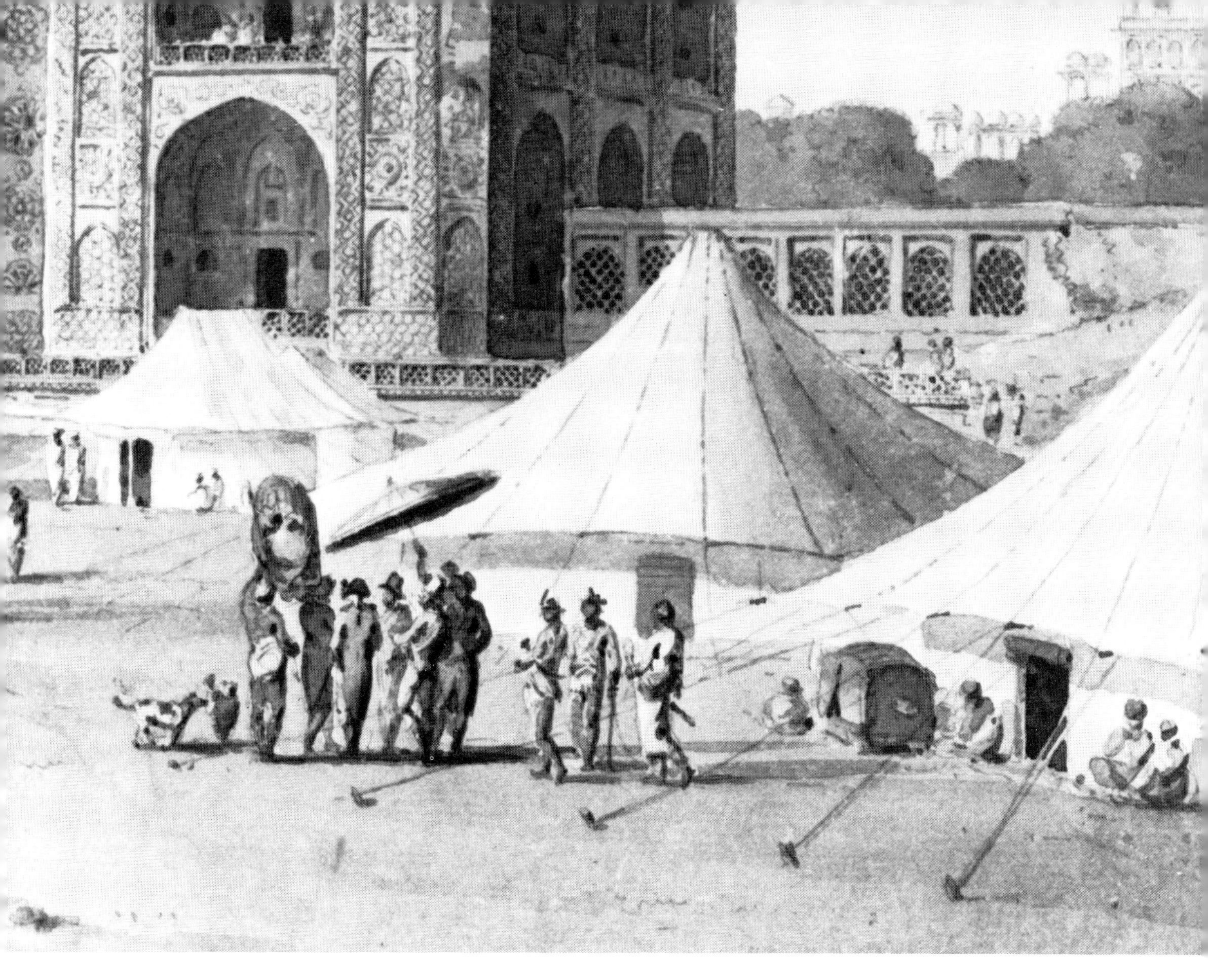

Some of the military party with whom the Daniells journeyed up-country, camped in front of Akbar's mausoleum at Sikandra: detail of the original watercolour for *no. 30*. In the left foreground are high-ranking officers, shaded by a parasol; next to them are Bengal sepoys, wearing 'sundial' turbans. A palanquin and its attendants wait outside the tent. (Private collection)

9 a.m. in order to keep warm. They travelled via Mahomedabad, Firozabad and Ahmedpur, admiring on the way the countryside with its fine groves of trees. They reached Agra on 20 January 1789 and their tents were pitched 'immediately opposite the Taj Mahal'.

At Agra the Daniells settled down to drawing with relentless enthusiasm (*nos. 27–29*). They spent the first day sketching the famous mausoleum and in the evening visited the tomb of Itimad-ud-Daula. Next morning they crossed the Jumna River and breakfasted in the Taj mosque with their old friend Major Palmer before drawing the inside of the Taj Mahal itself. Palmer was now the British Resident to the Maratha chief Sindhia who controlled the whole area. The day of 22 January was also spent drawing the Taj, Thomas working in the garden (*IV*) and William inside. In the evening the latter went up on to the dome and relaxed eating 'Apples Pears & Grapes of Persia from Major Palmers table'. The next two days were passed drawing the Red Fort. They compared Hodges' view with the original and William complained that 'like all his others' it was 'exceedingly faulty'. On 25 January they moved on to Sikandra to draw Akbar's mausoleum (*no. 30, V*), the road there reminding them of the Appian Way with ruins on both sides. Two days later the party reached Fatehpur Sikri,

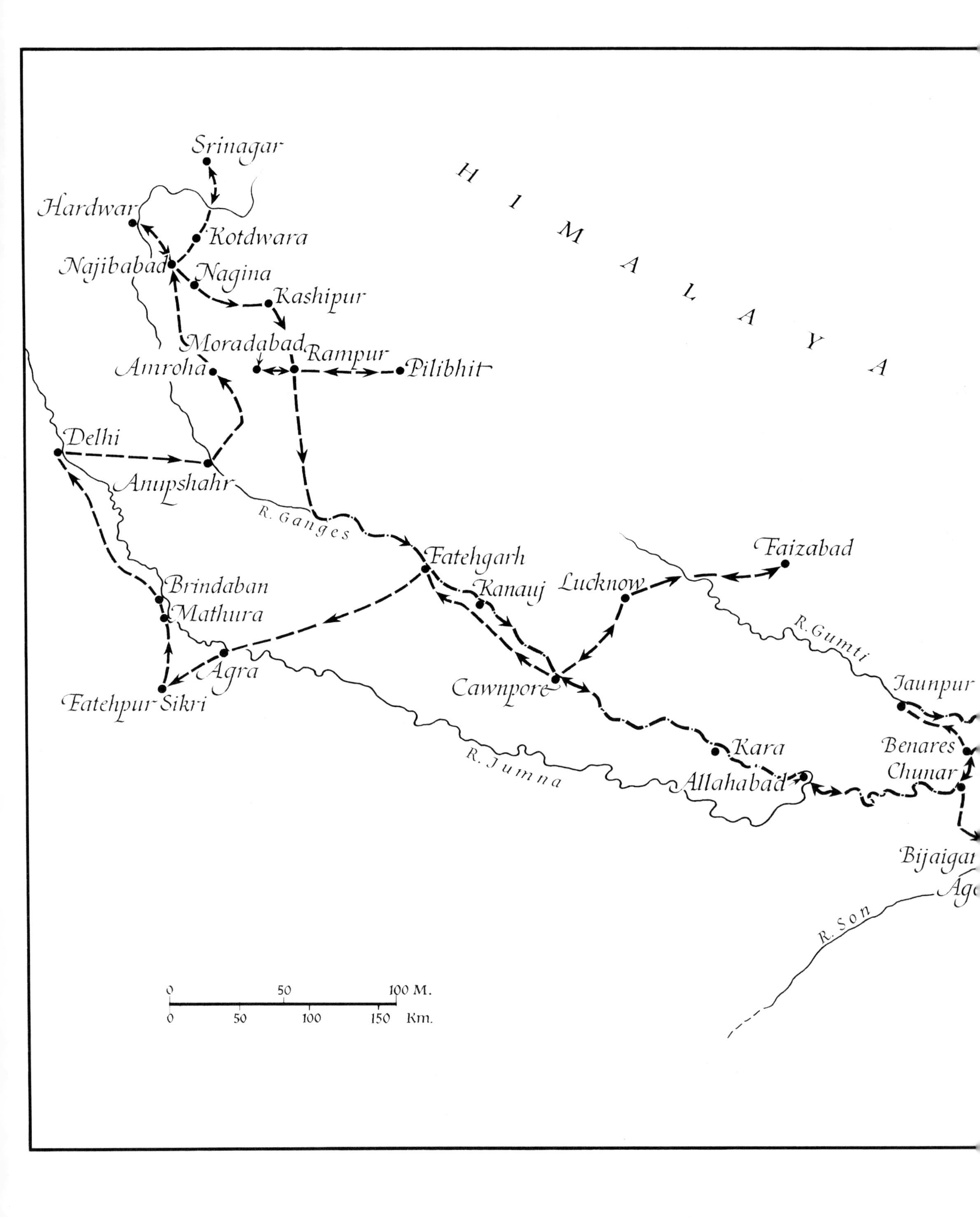

HIMALAYA
Srinagar
Hardwar
Kotdwara
Najibabad
Nagina
Kashipur
Moradabad
Rampur
Pilibhit
Amroha
Delhi
Anupshahr
R. Ganges
Fatehgarh
Faizabad
Lucknow
Kanauj
Brindaban
Mathura
Agra
Fatehpur Sikri
Cawnpore
R. Gumti
Jaunpur
Benares
Chunar
Kara
Allahabad
R. Jumna
Bijaigai
Ago
R. Son
0 50 100 M.
0 50 100 150 Km.

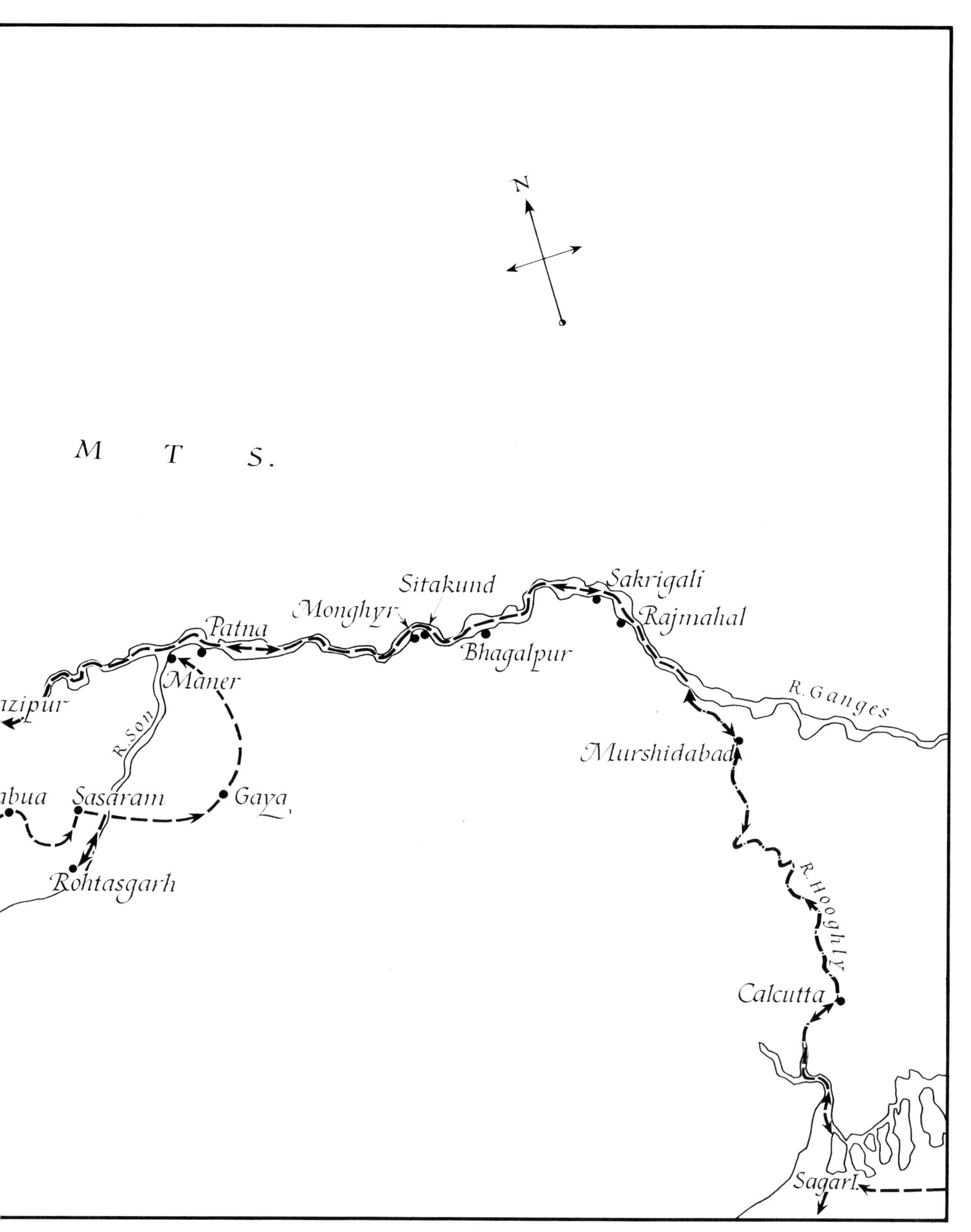

Map showing the Daniells' journey up-country to Srinagar (Part 2: aquatints *18–55*), and back down again to Calcutta via Lucknow (Part 3: aquatints *56–98*). The direction of movement is indicated by arrows – doubled where they went up and back by the same route.

A bullock cart, drawn in pencil by Thomas Daniell, with notes of its colours, *c.* 1789. (Private collection)

where the Daniells were particularly struck by the Buland Darwaza or Gate of Victory, which 'has an appearance of grandeur much superior to any thing we have seen in India the Tage not excepted'.

The journey was now becoming increasingly dangerous. On 30 January their camp was twice attacked by thieving Mewatis. The next day they halted at Aurangabad, 3 miles (some 5 kilometres) south of Mathura. The camp of the Maratha chief, Sindhia, was nearby and on 1 February they were introduced to him by Major Palmer. Thomas Daniell 'studied his Character pretty much & on our return made a sketch of his head', and later painted him 'from recollection'. Coming away they saw a dead Mewati in the road, his body left there as a warning to thieves. At Mathura (*no. 31*) they drew the river ghats and the fine mosque of Abd-un-Nabi before moving on to the holy city of Brindaban (*no. 32*). On 7 February they were very relieved to receive five dozen lead pencils sent from Fatehgarh, as their stock was running out.

The next objective was Delhi, which they reached on 16 February. They were now breaking new ground: Hodges had been unable to reach the city because of the Maratha menace. The city and its environs were so crowded with fine buildings and ruins that they were to stay there for two and half weeks (*nos. 33–43, VI, VII*). During this time the distinguished members of the party – Colonel Briscoe and Major Palmer – were received by the Mughal Emperor and the Daniells were invited to a nautch in Colonel Briscoe's tent. They worked hard, going from one building to another, seeing the palace-fortress, the various tombs and ruins as well as the early sites of the city known as the 'old Delhis'.

The hot season was now beginning and the Daniells planned to make for the Himalayas. On 6 March they set off to the east, moving through territory little known to the British. They were accompanied by four British officers and fifty sepoys. At Anupshahr they took part in a tiger hunt: William cleaned his gun and pistols in readiness for the great encounter but unfortunately he did not see a tiger and missed hitting a few hog deer. On 25 March they reached Najibabad (*no. 44*), having travelled through Sambhal, Amroha where there was a large *idgah* or Muslim prayer enclosure (see *no. 78*), and Chandpur with its fine travellers' rest-house. At Najibabad they were forced to wait for some days while arrangements were made through Jafar Khan, a local official, for permission to travel up into the hills to the little state of Srinagar in Garhwal. While they were waiting they made a few excursions towards the mountains and cross-examined some villagers, who had come down from the hills, concerning the country. They also visited Hardwar, the great pilgrimage city where the Ganges emerges from the hills. While there they were visited by the brother-in-law of the Srinagar Raja. All this time they could see the lower ranges of the Himalayas on the skyline and their excitement was mounting.

Accompanied by two officers, Captain Guthrie and Lieutenant Sturmer, the Daniells at last set off from Najibabad on 18 April and marched to Kotdwara (*no. 45, VIII*) at the foot of the hills. Here they collected coolies for the trek and prepared their *jampans* or carrying chairs. Four days later they began to follow the Khoh River on their journey to Srinagar. It was often too steep to use their *jampans* and they had to clamber up the rocky watercourse (*no. 46*). They camped the first night at Jhawanu ('Jugeanor', *no. 47*) where they were delighted to see stinging nettles for the first time since leaving England. The next day they reached Diosa ('Dusa', *no. 48*), where conifers began to appear in the woods and William picked yellow raspberries for a pudding. On 24 April they climbed higher still and obtained superb views although they could not see the snows because of the haze. To their right Languri Fort ('Lungor') was visible. They dropped 12 miles (20 kilometres) down to the narrow river valley of the Ramganga between Bilkhet and Badel (*no. 49*). The scenery and villages with their wooden houses (*no. 50*) reminded them of the watercolours of Bhutan which Samuel Davis had shown them (p. 39). They found many plants similar to English ones growing wild. On 25 April they reached Naithana ('Natan') and the next day they obtained a glorious view of the snows (*no. 51, IX*), whose height far exceeded all expectations. They camped that night near Takandhar ('Taka Ca Munda', *no. 52*) and the next day ascended even higher, the snows reappearing. An exhausting march followed as they climbed down to the Kandha River and then up again (*no. 53*). Here they enjoyed a fine panorama of Srinagar and the Alakananda River before descending once more and pitching their tent south-west of the town.

Raja Pradhyumna Shah of Garhwal seated against a bolster, with his younger brother, Parakram, beside him. It was at his court that delicate miniatures were painted depicting the exploits of Krishna and the moods of lovers. This drawing was made by a Garhwal artist about 1785. (Tehri Raj Collection, Garhwal)

Three eventful days were passed at Srinagar. They were the first Europeans to visit the area. As soon as they arrived on the 27th the local people flocked around to gaze at them. In the evening the local Raja, Pradhyumna Shah (ruled (1785–1804), and his brother paid them a visit, accompanied by drums and trumpets. The party crowded into the tent and the Raja was presented with a watch and two pistols. The next morning the ruler's attendants came to warn them that they were in some danger. The Raja, they learned, was involved in a war with his younger brother Parakram, Raja of the neighbouring state of Kumaon to the south. The latter had been victorious and was now pursuing the remnants of the Srinagar army. In about two hours they might arrive. The English party preserved an air of calm unconcern. They set out to examine the rope bridge across the river and the two Daniells made drawings of it (*no. 54*).

The bridge was crowded with the local people fleeing with their baggage from the pursuing army, which however did not appear. William was very pleased with the gifts which the Raja's people brought to them – three beautiful birds, some musk and a yak's tail. The next day they were again visited by the Raja, who ostensibly came to ask how the watch and the pistols worked. Captain Guthrie gave some gunpowder to one of the attendants who in experimenting with it broke his matchlock and injured his shoulder. The Raja seemed ill at ease all the time and at last it emerged that he had really come to ask Captain Guthrie if he and his party would assist him in repulsing the Kumaon forces. The British group prudently decided it was now time to withdraw, and on 30 April they left Srinagar early in the morning. Halfway up the hill they stopped for Thomas and William to make final drawings of the valley below. They returned to the plains by a slightly different route, a little to the east of the way they had come. As they went they could see fires burning in the distance where the Kumaon Raja was raiding villages.

On 3 May they reached Dadamandi at the junction of the Bhairan and Pawai Rivers (*no.* 55). Here they found raspberries and wild cherries and Thomas kept some of the cherry stones to take back to Samuel Davis who was a keen horticulturist. They cut back to Jhawanu and from there they descended to the plains by the same route as before. It was not until 1796, when Captain Thomas Hardwicke made a tour there, that a European was again to set foot in Garhwal.

1 (19)

II (24)

III (26)

IV (28)

v (30)

vi (42)

vii (40) >

VIII (45)

IX (51)

18

18 'Near Bandell on the River Hoogly' (IV, *Twenty-Four Landscapes*, 8)

7 September 1788. 'Weighed at 6 o C, passed Chinsurah at 9, Hooghley at 10 & Bandell at 11. Just as we passed the last mentioned Place a fine Breeze sprung up & carried us to the upper end of Jerbony sand when suddenly it fell Calm & we with difficulty got round the Point. We anchored abt 2 Miles [3 km] on this side of Nia-serai Creek. Made many Sketches in the course of the Day. Ther 83 [28.3 °C].' (*Journal*)

'Temples and other sacred structures of the Hindoos', writes Thomas Daniell in his note on this plate, 'occur frequently on the banks of the Hoogley; and these buildings, of various forms, and in different situations, exposed or half concealed among deep and solemn groves, no less holy in the popular opinion, than the edifices they shelter, give an air of romantic grandeur . . .

The small monumental erection in the centre of this view, as well as the obelisk near it, rudely carved in wood, are called Suttees; and though possessed of no sculptural elegance, are most curious memorials of the perversion of human intellect, having been raised to commemmorate the immolation of certain unfortunate females, who, in compliance with a horrid custom among Hindoos, had been induced to give the last dreadful proof of conjugal fidelity, by a voluntary death on the funeral pile of their deceased husbands.' This custom, incomprehensible 'among a people distinguished for their mild and inoffensive manners', had, Thomas comments with relief, been prohibited in territories governed by the British.

19

19 'Mausoleum of Nawaub Assoph Khan, Rajemahel' (III, *Oriental Scenery*, 24). *See also colour plate I*

9 October 1788. 'Went to Rajimal in our Palanquins where we met the Pinnace – passed thro' the Caravanserai that Hodges has made an Aquatinta print of – walked about the Ruins of Rajimal & saw many very Picturesque Views indeed. There was great trouble in getting the Boats round the old pieces of Building that had fell into the River as the current ran with an amazing swiftness. Saw many Alligators of a very large kind in the River.' (*Journal*)

From 1592 to 1607 and again from 1639 to 1707 Rajmahal was the capital of Bihar and Bengal, and the ruins of many fine buildings remained. When Thomas Skinner visited the spot in 1826 he noted, 'it was a complete wilderness, and as the rooms would afford admirable shelter to robbers, so might the courts to tigers and snakes.' The Daniells particularly admired the 'glazed tiles of various designs and colours' with which the tombs and palaces were decorated. 'These porcelain embellishments were often applied with great taste, and from the richness of their colours and enamelled surface, produced a very splendid effect.'

The artists appear to have been given inaccurate information about this particular tomb: Asaf Khan, the Mughal Governor of Bengal in 1608, had built a mansion at Rajmahal but had not died there, and the mausoleum is more likely that of his brother, Ibrahim Khan.

20 'Siccra Gulley on the Ganges' (IV, *Twenty-Four Landscapes*, 9)

October 1788. Sakrigali, situated at the foot of a pass into the adjoining hills, was a favourite spot for boats to anchor. 'At this place', writes Thomas Daniell, 'is commonly an assemblage of small vessels, which, together with the craft of various descriptions that appear scattered over the surface of this widely extended river, produce a most impressive effect of commercial activity.' The scene was 'perfectly enchanting; hills finely varied, buildings interspersed, a luxuriant vegetation, and the whole illumined by a bright and serene atmosphere . . . The small building upon the lower eminence is a bungalo, or cottage, belonging to the British resident of the Bhagulpore district, and placed here for his occasional use, either to transact public business, or to accommodate himself or friends, when they repair hither to enjoy the amusements of the country.'

When Fanny Parks' pinnace anchored there in November 1844, the bungalow was occupied by a French indigo planter who kept tigers. It would, she observed, 'be an excellent shooting box', for game of all kinds abounded in the area – birds, tigers, bears, leopards, rhinoceroses, deer and hogs.

20

21 'Part of the City of Patna, on the River Ganges' (I, *Oriental Scenery*, 10)

8 November 1788. 'The large and populous City of Patna is in the province of Bahar. The gauts, or steps leading up from the river, are very numerous here, and are intended for the advantage of merchandise, as well as the convenience of the Hindoos, whose religious duties oblige them frequently to perform ablutions in the sacred river Ganges.

The larger building is the house of an Hindoo merchant, and is an example of the general style of buildings on the river side inhabited by men of that class.'

Patna, site of the ancient city of Pataliputra, was a prosperous trading centre exporting sugar, lac, cotton, indigo, musk from Bhutan and saltpetre for gunpowder. The Dutch, French and British all had factories there built along the river, the latter dealing largely in calicoes and chintzes. When James Forbes visited the city in 1785 he noted that from the river it made 'a good appearance. There we found a number of vessels employed in its commerce, and the bazaar well stocked with merchandise, particularly abounding with coppersmiths, cooks and confectioners.' Thomas Twining in 1794 was struck by the wealth of the local gentry: 'There was an unmixed genuineness of manners accompanied with a profusion of show and parade, to which the streets of Madras and Calcutta offered nothing similar . . . The rich inhabitants seemed to reside in the part between the great street and the river. I here saw several palaces of extensive but irregular and inelegant construction.'

21

22 'The Mausoleum of Mucdoom Shah Dowlut, at Moneah, on the River Soane' (I, *Oriental Scenery*, 12)

13 November 1788. 'Past the village Surpoor abt 10 0 C. & brought too about 4 close to the River Soane. We went on shore & walked to a Mosque at Moneah a little beyond the Bazar. (Hodges has made Drawings &c from it.) It is one of the highest finished pieces of Architecture we have seen in the Country, built entirely of Stone.' (*Journal*)

The Muslim saint, Makhdam Shah Daulat, had died in 1608 and was interred at Maner, a village near the junction of the rivers Son and Ganges, 25 miles (40 km) west of Patna. His mausoleum was later erected by a disciple. Hodges had been particularly attracted by it, and in his *Travels* he noted: 'This building though not large is certainly very beautiful: it is a square with pavilions rising from the angles; and in the center is a majestic dome, the top of which is finished by what the Indian architects call a cullus: the line of the curve of the dome is not broken, but is continued by an inverted curve until it finishes in a crescent. I cannot but greatly prefer this to the manner in which all great domes are finished in Europe, by erecting a small building on the top, which, at the point of contact with the dome, has a sharp angle.'

22

23 'Ramnugur near Benares on the Ganges' (I, *Oriental Scenery*, 14) *5 December 1788*. 'Sailed by Ramnagur with a fine Wind abt 9 o C, but were soon obliged to lower the sails, the Wind blowing strong ahead of us.' (*Journal*)

'Ramnagur is a fort built by Raja Bulwunt Sing, and considerably improved by his son Cheyt Sing.'

The fort was of great interest to the Daniells since it was the scene of a frightening incident in August 1781 when Warren Hastings and his party, amongst whom was the artist William Hodges, almost lost their lives (see pp. 99–100).

The British often stopped at Ramnagar; the more eminent were frequently invited to visit the Rajah, but the Daniells were not in that category. Emily Eden, sister of the Governor-General Lord Auckland, describes setting off on her visit on 22 November 1837. 'The Rajah of Benares asked us to come to his country-house, called Ramnuggur. It is on the other side of the Ganges . . . We found the rajah's boats waiting for us – a silver armchair and footstool for his lordship in the prow; which was decorated with silvered peacocks, and a sort of red embroidered tent for 'his women', where we placed ourselves, though there was another boat with two inferior silver chairs for F. [Fanny] and me.'

24 'The Chalees Satoon in the Fort of Allahabad on the River Jumna' (I, *Oriental Scenery*, 6). *See also colour plate II*

17 December 1788. 'Spent most of the Day passing Allahabad. Were obliged to unload the Boat as the people thought there would be great danger in getting her through the strong Water. Got eight or ten Men to assist us, when we went thro' very well – brought too above the Fort.' (*Journal*)

The palace-fortress at Allahabad, at the junction of the Jumna and the Ganges, was begun by Akbar in 1583 and was the largest fort built by him. The Chalis Satun ('Hall of Forty Pillars') was built as a pleasure pavilion in the palace, situated high up beside the river so that the cool breezes could circulate throughout. Such pavilions had no walls; water ran through channels in the building and fountains played around it. Fanny Parks (1836) remarked of a similar structure at Ghazipur, 'Imagine the luxury of sitting in the centre room, all the air coming in cooled by the fountains, and screened from the glare by the rich pardas [curtains].'

24

25 'Near the Fort of Currah, on the River Ganges' (III, *Oriental Scenery*, 1)
20 December 1788. 'From Shawpour to Currah the Banks are exceedingly picturesque, spotted with a great Variety of Building.' (*Journal*)

'The Fort of Currah was formerly of considerable importance. It is situated on high ground on the western bank of the River Ganges . . . The buildings on the water side are appropriated to the religious purposes of the Hindoos.'

Kara was a sacred place in early Hindu days. It was conquered by the Muslims in 1194 and became a seat of government until the present fort and city of Allahabad were built by Akbar in 1583 as the new administrative centre. Ruins of the old city extended along the river bank for 2 miles (3 km) and provided the Daniells with many attractive subjects.

26

26 'Near Currah, on the River Ganges' (I, *Oriental Scenery*, 21). *See also colour plate III*
20 December 1788. In this aquatint Thomas Daniell catches the great beauty of the Ganges in the cold weather with its smooth surface and high banks which in the rains crumble and fall into the stream. He was interested in the little shrine which, he says, 'although built for the worship of Hindoo idols, is almost wholly in the Mahommedan style of design, as indeed are many other modern Hindoo temples'.

When Lord Valentia passed the same spot in 1803 he too was attracted by the temples and tombs. 'I was tempted', he wrote, 'by the appearance of several picturesque pagodas overshadowed by tamarinds and banyan trees to land at a gaut, and visit one of the largest, where was an image of Mahadeo [Shiva] in the centre, and the bull looking at him.'

At this time, before the coming of the railways, transport was largely by water and country boats with their great sails were continually passing. The *Oriental Annual* of 1837 describes these boats: 'The deck is a floor of bamboos, placed close together, and united by cords of coir, a description of rope manufactured from the husk of the cocoanut . . . They carry a large square sail of thin light canvas, upon a pliant bamboo yard, which is lowered with great facility at the slightest indication of stormy weather.'

27 'The Taje Mahel, at Agra' (I, *Oriental Scenery*, 18)
20 January 1789. 'Started abt 6 o C. & reached Agra by 9 . . .
21 January. Crossed the Jumna abt 7 o C. & breakfasted with Major Palmer in one of the Mosques in the Tage. After breakfast we all visited the inside of the Tage & were much struck with its Magnificent Workmanship.
22 January. Spent the Whole Day at the Tage Mahl. Un. drew the View from the Garden in the Camera – myself employed on the inside. In the evening went upon the Dome. Eat of some Apples Pears & Grapes of Persia from Major Palmers table.' (*Journal*)

The Taj Mahal was raised by the Mughal Emperor, Shah Jahan, as a mausoleum for his favourite wife, known as Mumtaz-i-Mahal, 'The Elect of the Palace', who died in 1629. Shah Jahan, it is said, planned a similar tomb for himself of black marble, across the river, but after his death he was interred beside her.

There is little doubt that in spite of his deep interest in Hindu architecture, Thomas Daniell, like so many Europeans after him, preferred the Mughal style. It seems somewhat strange therefore that in *Oriental Scenery* he only produced this one view of the Taj, showing the gateway with the mausoleum in the background. 'The Gate', he comments, 'is of red stone and white marble, elegantly ornamented. The Spandrels over the arches are decorated with foliage of various coloured stones inlaid.'

He was probably criticized for not showing the mausoleum in greater detail, with the result that in 1801 he produced the two lavish prints that follow.

27

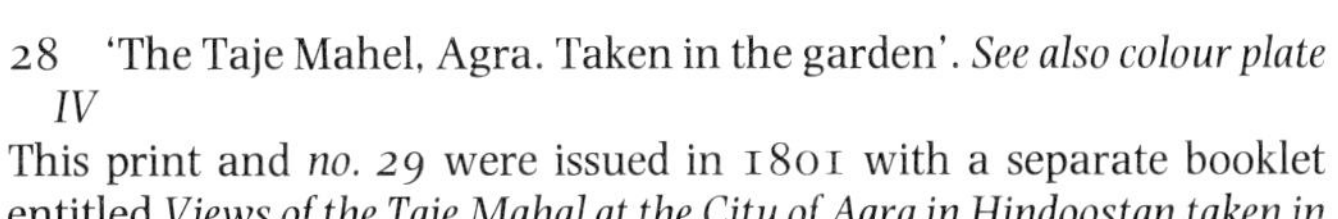

28 'The Taje Mahel, Agra. Taken in the garden'. *See also colour plate IV*

This print and *no. 29* were issued in 1801 with a separate booklet entitled *Views of the Taje Mahal at the City of Agra in Hindoostan taken in 1789*. They are nearly 3 feet (90 cm) wide, even larger than the plates of *Oriental Scenery*. The booklet included a ground plan of the whole area, engraved by James Newton, with detailed references to the various parts of the building. 'The Taje Mahel', Thomas Daniell observed, 'has always been considered as the first example of Mahomedan architecture in India, and consequently, being a spectacle of the highest celebrity, is visited by persons of all rank, and from all parts. This high admiration is however not confined to the partial eye of the native Indian; it is beheld with no less wonder and delight by those who have seen the productions of art in various parts of the globe.'

22 January 1789. As William's diary records (see *no. 27*), Thomas made a first drawing of the Taj from the garden with the help of the camera obscura.

'The garden view of the Taje Mahel was taken immediately on entering it by the principal gate . . . whence the Mausoleum, being seen down an avenue of trees, has on first entering a most impressive effect on the spectator. The large marble bason in the centre of the garden with fountains, and those rising out of the watery channel with paved walks on each side, add to the variety and richness of the scene, and give to it that coolness which is so luxurious an improvement to an Oriental garden.'

It is clear that the garden had deteriorated with the decline of the Mughal Empire. Great trees had been allowed to grow up in place of the small trim parterres so beloved by the Mughals. These would have been filled with brightly coloured or scented flowers – tuberoses, marigolds, poppies, balsam and cockscomb. When Hodges had visited the Taj six years earlier he found the garden in 'tolerable repair' and the fountains played for him.

28

29

29 'The Taje Mahel, Agra' *See no. 28*
20 January 1789. '... The Tents were pitched immediately opposite the Tage Mahl. Un & self drawing from it most of the Day.' (*Journal*)

Hodges, like the Daniells, had been greatly impressed by the view across the river. 'The whole', he wrote, 'appears like a most perfect pearl on an azure ground. The effect is such, I confess, I never experienced from any work of art.' The romantic Fanny Parks, after her visit in 1835, echoed the sentiments of most British visitors: 'And now Adieu, beautiful Taj, adieu! In the far, far West I shall rejoice that I have gazed upon your beauty nor will the memory depart until the lowly tomb of an English gentlewoman closes on my remains.'

In the present century, sophisticated British taste has at times swung against Muslim architecture in favour of Hindu. The Taj made little impression on E. M. Forster, and Aldous Huxley in *Jesting Pilate* (1926) put an extreme view. He found the architecture dry and negative, 'the product of a deficiency of fancy, a poverty of imagination', and the minarets 'among the ugliest structures ever created by human hands'.

30

30 'Gate of the Tomb of the Emperor Akbar at Secundra, near Agra' (I, *Oriental Scenery*, 9). *See also colour plate V and p. 43*
25 January 1789. 'Left Agra abt 6 o C. & arrived at our Ground at Secundra . . . abt 8 o C. Un. employed the Whole Day drawing the Gates (in the Camera) leading to the Tomb of Akbar. The Road from Agra to Secundar affords many fine Views. It is covered with Buildings & Ruins the Whole way. The Whole put one in mind of the Appian Way on account of the numerous remains of considerable buildings.' (*Journal*)

The print gives a clear idea of the manner in which the Daniells travelled during this stage of their journey when they had attached themselves to a party bound for Agra. A large encampment of tents is set up just outside the main gateway and the scene is busy with the British, their servants and bodyguard.

The mausoleum had been built by Akbar's son, Jahangir, and was completed in 1613. Thomas Twining visited it in 1794 and noted that the gate 'resembled in many respects the grand entrance to the garden of the Taje,' but excelled it 'in having beautiful minarets of white marble at the four angles of the building, though about two-thirds alone of these ornaments now remained, the upper parts having been struck and thrown down by lightning. . . . The exterior is highly wrought and inlaid with stones of different colours. This gateway is considered one of the finest monuments in Hindostan.'

The minarets, which have now been restored, are architecturally significant since this was the first time in Northern India that they had been used in this fashion on a mausoleum.

31 'View of Mutura, on the River Jumna' (III, *Oriental Scenery*, 22)
2 February 1789. 'This view of the ancient town of Mutura is taken from a garden on the opposite of the river Jumna, somewhat elevated, in which there is a handsome pavilion carefully executed in the modern Mahomedan style.'

The engraving shows the fort in the centre and to the left the mosque of Abd-un-Nabi which had been built by the bigoted Mughal Emperor Aurangzeb on the site of an ancient Hindu temple. The act was especially obnoxious since Mathura was an important centre of Hindu pilgrimage, believed, on the basis of a prophecy in the Bhagavata Purana, to be the birthplace of Krishna, an incarnation of the god Vishnu (see *no. 32*).

31

32

32 'Hindoo Temples at Bindrabund on the River Jumna' (I, *Oriental Scenery*, 2)

10 February 1789. From Mathura the Daniells proceeded to Brindaban, another sacred city, where Krishna spent his childhood. When he was born at Mathura, the god Vishnu appeared to his parents and bade them to smuggle the child at once to nearby Brindaban so that he could escape the vengeance of Raja Kansa, who was terrifying the kingdom and banning the worship of Vishnu. He was quickly taken to the house of a herdsman, Nanda, and exchanged for the baby girl who had just been born to Nanda's wife, Yasoda. It was here that Krishna grew up and passed an idyllic boyhood amongst the cowherds of Braj before he returned to Mathura to fulfill the prophecy by killing Raja Kansa.

Brindaban like Mathura became a place of pilgrimage. Temples were built beside the River Jumna across which the baby Krishna had been carried at night. Thomas Daniell was greatly impressed by these 'beautiful & singular Pagodas. They are most elegantly sculptured; certain carved ribs go equidistant into small figures prettily filled with rosettes.' When Thomas returned to England he submitted an oil painting of these temples as his Diploma picture for the Royal Academy, where it still hangs.

Humphry Repton used this aquatint in his design of 1806 for an aviary for the Royal Pavilion at Brighton, wittily transforming the massive sandstone tower or shikara into a fairy-like open structure (ill. p. 232). Hindu temples of this shape became symbolic of India, and one appears in an 'exotic' French wallpaper of 1815 (see p. 230).

33

33 'The Mausoleum of Amir Khusero, at the Ancient City of Delhi' (III, *Oriental Scenery*, 6)

16 February 1789. After reaching their camping ground on the outskirts of Delhi, the Daniells the same evening visited the tomb of the famous early fourteenth-century saint Shaikh Nizam-ud-Din Aulia. They greatly admired the mausoleum of the celebrated Delhi poet Amir Khusrau which was situated to the south of the enclosure containing the tomb of the Saint.

'This Mausoleum is built of white marble, finely polished and finished with the utmost delicacy; particularly the lattice work, which is introduced on each side of it.'

In the foreground is a litter of the type used by Indian gentlemen, as distinct from the box palanquin favoured by the British.

34 'A Baolee near the Old City of Delhi' (III, *Oriental Scenery*, 18)
16 February 1789. While visiting the tomb of Nizam-ud-Din Aulia, the Daniells saw nearby a large stepped well or *baoli*, which had been built by the Saint's followers and was considered sacred by them. 'On the top of the wall to the right, were fixed conveniences for drawing water, which is generally performed by bullocks walking down an inclined plane, and by means of a rope fastened to a strong leathern bucket the water is raised up.' (*Journal*)

35 'The Jummah Musjed, Delhi' (I, *Oriental Scenery*, 23)
36 'Eastern Gate of the Jummah Musjid at Delhi': *see overleaf*
18 February 1789. 'We breakfasted very early & spent the Day at the Jummaigh Musjid, built by Shah Jehan. Un employed in the Camera, took a view of the Mosque with the Minorets.' (*Journal*)

Situated to the west of the Red Fort, the Jami Masjid was built by Shah Jahan in 1650–56. It is the largest mosque in India, its enclosure dramatically built up (*no.* 35) and punctuated by three gateways. The minarets and domed prayer-hall, seen here, are striped and variously ornamented in pale marble and deep red sandstone.

E. M. Forster, during his last visit to India in 1945, described his feelings on standing in this vast courtyard – shoeless, as in all mosques. 'Next day I stood on the high platform of the Great Mosque, one of the noblest buildings in India and the world. Profound thankfulness filled me. The sky was now intensely blue, the kites circled round and round the pearl-grey domes and the red frontispiece of sandstone, sounds drifted up from Delhi city, the pavement struck warm through the soles of my socks; I was back in the country I loved after an absence of twenty-five years.'

37 'North East View of the Cotsea Bhaug, on the River Jumna, Delhi' (I, *Oriental Scenery*, 3)
22 February 1789. 'Cotsea Bhaug, so called from the bhaug, or garden, within the quadrangular building, which was erected by the Cotsea Begum, a Mahommedan lady, in the reign of the Emperor Akbar, about two hundred years since. . . . The apartments receive light principally from the garden side, excepting the octangular projections at the angles.'

The print is of particular interest since this 'quadrangular building' enclosing the Qudsia Bagh has now completely disappeared. It formed the eastern bastion of the Red Fort, a gateway of which can be seen in the far distance.

In 1806 Repton based part of his design for the Royal Pavilion at Brighton on his building (ill. p. 232). Mughal marble lattice work appealed to British architects of the early nineteenth century.

34

^
35

37

36 'Eastern gate of the Jummah Musjid at Delhi' (I, *Oriental Scenery*, 1)

18 February 1789. Shah Jahan's great mosque (see *no. 36*, overleaf) stands on a high platform on a rock and is approached by flights of steps up to gateways on the north, south and east, the latter – shown here – being the main entrance. In his note Thomas Daniell comments: 'The materials are of reddish stone, brought from the neighbouring Mewat hills, and white Cashmerian marble. The spires on the small domes are gilt. The folding doors are covered with brass, very neatly ornamented with a regular design in basso relievo. The whole is of excellent workmanship.'

Emily Eden in her journal, *Up the Country* (1838), described this mosque as 'the finest we have yet seen. It is in such perfect preservation, built entirely of red stone and white marble, with immense flights of steps leading up to three sides of it; these, the day we went to it, were entirely covered with people dressed in very bright colours – Sikhs and Mahrattas, and some of the fair Mogul race, all assembled to see the Governor General's suwarree [procession], and I do not think I ever saw so striking a scene. They followed us into the court of the temple, which is surmounted by an open arched gallery, and through every arch there was a view of some fine ruins, or of some part of the King of Delhi's palace, . . . all built of deep red stone.'

The grandeur of the Jami Masjid greatly attracted the British and it is not surprising that the Daniells chose this subject for the very first print of *Oriental Scenery*, published in March 1795.

38

38 'The Western Entrance of Shere Shah's Fort, Delhi' (I, *Oriental Scenery*, 13)
24 February 1789. 'Marched this morning to Old Delhi abt 13 Miles [21 km] SW of the Fort built by Shah Jehan.' (*Journal*)

The Old Fort or Purana Qila was built by the Afghan ruler Sher Shah Sur after he secured the throne at Delhi in 1540. It was raised over the mound which is said to contain the remains of the ancient city of Indraprastha associated with the epic of the *Mahabharata*. Its ramparts cover an area of over 2 miles (3 km) and it has three main gates on the north, south and west. Built of red sandstone, the gates are two-storeyed and are surmounted by small kiosks or chhatris. The remains of a moat can be seen which connected up with the Jumna River on one side of the fort.

39, 40 'The Observatory at Delhi' (V, *Antiquities of India*, 20 and 19). *See also colour plate VII*
24 February 1789. The Jantar-Mantar was one of a series of observatories raised at Delhi, Jaipur, Ujjain, Benares and Mathura in about 1724 by Maharaja Jai Singh II of Jaipur, on instructions from the Mughal Emperor, Muhammad Shah, to reform the Hindu calendar.

39

In the 1780s and 1790s a number of the British were taking a keen interest in Indian astronomy and were publishing articles in *Asiatic Researches*, the lively journal of the Asiatic Society of Bengal, of which Thomas Daniell was a member. While he and William were exploring the Jantar-Mantar their friend Samuel Davis in Bhagalpur was writing an article, 'On the Astronomical computations of the Hindus' (published in *Asiatic Researches*, II, 1799), and he must already have been working on this material when they stayed with him in October 1788.

Thomas Daniell was clearly fascinated by the shapes of the observatory instruments, especially the great equatorial dial seen from opposite directions in these two prints, and remarked in his comment, 'Should it be thought these extraordinary works ought not to have been classed with the Antiquities of India . . . the Author hopes that the singularity, as well as the magnitude of such astronomical instruments, will be a sufficient apology for introducing them here.' The word 'singularity' is significant. This was a quality which in England became an aesthetic category of Romantic landscape. Usually the term was applied to natural phenomena such as rocks and monoliths but there seems little doubt that Thomas Daniell was regarding these strange instruments in a similar way as impressive abstract shapes.

40

41

42

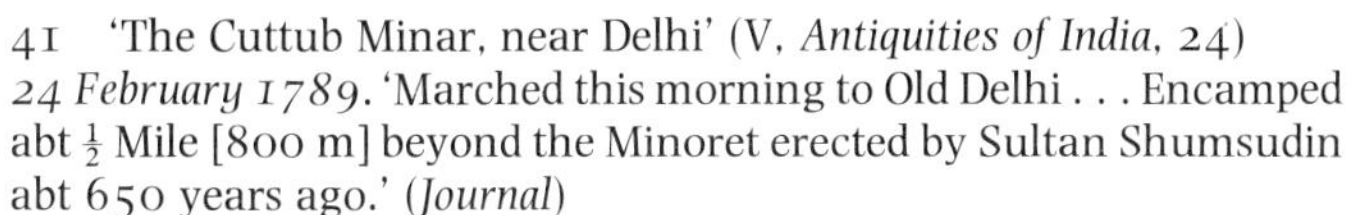

41 'The Cuttub Minar, near Delhi' (V, *Antiquities of India*, 24)
24 February 1789. 'Marched this morning to Old Delhi . . . Encamped abt ½ Mile [800 m] beyond the Minoret erected by Sultan Shumsudin abt 650 years ago.' (*Journal*)

The Qutb Minar, the foundations of which were laid by Qutb-ud-Din Aibak in 1199, was probably intended both as a tower of victory, to celebrate the Muslim Afghans' defeat of the Rajputs, and as a minar for the cry to prayer of the nearby Quwwat-ul-Islam ('Might of Islam') mosque. The tower was not finished by Qutb-ud-Din and the upper storeys were added by his successor Iltutmish. Repairs were made by later rulers. The three first storeys are of red sandstone and the upper stages are partly faced with white marble. In 1803 an earthquake shattered the top seen here and it was replaced by Colonel Robert Smith, an engineer and amateur artist. His finial was highly controversial, however; in 1848 it was taken down, and it now stands at the foot of the minar to the south-east.

Emily Eden, who could be very sour about India, was enthusiastic about the Qutb Minar. In a letter of 23 February 1838 she wrote, 'Well of all the things I ever saw, I think this is the finest. Did we know about it in England? I mean, did you and I, in our old ancient Briton state, know? . . . Don't be ashamed, there is no harm in not knowing, only I do say it is rather a pity we were so ill taught . . . It happens to be the Monument [to the Great Fire of London] put at the top of the column in the Place Vendome and that again placed on a still grander base. It is built of beautiful red granite, is 240 feet [73 m] high and 50 feet [15 m] in diameter, and carved all over with sentences from the Koran, each letter a yard [90 cm] high, and the letter again interlaced and ornamented with carved flowers and garlands; it is between six and seven hundred years old, and looks as if it were finished yesterday, and it stands in a wilderness of ruins, carved gateways, and marble tombs, one more beautiful than the other.'

42 'Remains of an Ancient Building near Firoz Shah's Cotilla, Delhi' (I, *Oriental Scenery*, 7). *See also colour plate VI*
1 March 1789. 'About a mile [1.6 km] to the W of our Camp on a small hill lay in Ruins a Minoret erected by Firozshah. It lay near the Ruins of an old Building built in the time of Firoz shah by a Patan – from the top of it I made a general View of Delhi. Saw abt 6 feet [2 m] below the surface of the earth Human Skeletons as thick as they possibly could be put together abt ½ a mile [800 m] from the Jumna, where I suppose there had been once a bloody battle.' (*Journal*)

The fifth city of Delhi was built by Firuz Shah Tughluq (ruled 1351–88) on the banks of the Jumna. The ruins of the citadel, the Kotla Firuz Shah, now lie south-east of modern Delhi on the Mathura road as the Jumna has shifted its course further east. The buildings shown in the aquatint have disappeared.

This print was one chosen by Staffordshire potters to decorate the dish reproduced on p. 228.

43 'View at Delhi, near the Mausoleum of Humaioon' (III, *Oriental Scenery*, 19)

5 March 1789. The Daniells had begun the day sketching in the Red Fort, but 'the people flocked about so thick & were so very troublesome that I think we should not have been able to have drawn any more in the fort. Set off immediately to Humaion's tomb where we made a few Sketches.' (*Journal*)

'The Mausoleum of the emperor Humaioon is within the high wall to the left. This view consists principally of mausoleums, and the magnificent gateways that lead to the gardens in which they are placed. These buildings are of stone; the domes in general, and many other parts have been covered with porcelain tiles of various colours, ornamented with a great display of richness and elegance, of which many examples are still remaining.'

The mausoleum of Humayun – the second Mughal emperor, and father of Akbar – was built by his widow after his death in 1556. It is the first mature example of a garden-tomb.

This print showing the plain covered with ruins explains the sober reveries of so many of the British in Delhi. As Charles Metcalfe, Assistant Resident at Delhi in 1806, wrote, 'There is, however, something in this place to which the mind cannot be indifferent. The ruins of grandeur that extend for miles on every side fill it with serious reflection. The palaces crumbling into dust, every one of which could tell many tales of royal virtue or tyrannical crime, of desperate ambition or depraved indolence . . . the myriads of vast mausoleums, every one of which was intended to convey to futurity the deathless fame of its cold inhabitant, and all of which are passed by unknown and unnoticed . . . these things cannot be looked at with indifference.'

44 'View at Nijeibabad, near the Coaduwar Gaut, Rohilcund' (IV, *Twenty-Four Landscapes*, 13)
16 April 1789. 'Had a very agreeable short march to Nidjibabad [Najibabad] abt 8 miles [13 km] SSW thro' a pleasant country – saw many herd of Deer on our march but they were so very shy that it was impossible to get within Gun Shot. Propose leaving this for Coudwar Gaut the day after tomorrow. . . .
17 April. Halted to-day . . . attempted to make our Chairs into hill Palanquins but without success – however fastened my Chair to Bamboos in such manner as to be able to march in it on a plain.' (*Journal*)

'Nigeibabad is one of the most opulent towns in the fertile district of Rohilcund, and subject at this time to Fizula Cawn. It is a place of tolerable trade, chiefly carried on with the mountainous country in its vicinity, whence a variety of ores, gums, and spices are brought and disposed of in the bazars, of which there are several.'

45 'Coaduwar Gaut' (IV, *Twenty-Four Landscapes*, 14). *See also colour plate VIII*
18 April 1789. 'Un, self, Capt. Guthrie & Lieut. Sturmer left Nidgebabad abt 5 o C, & . . . were overtaken by Golaum Mahommed who accompanied us to Coadwar Gaut, where we received very great attention from the people of the Place.
19 April. In the evening the Fouzdar brought us some Jampans or hill Palanquins, but fearing they would be too slight Un began to make one for himself.
20 April. Spent most of the Day making Jampans &c for tomorrows march – part of the day both washing our Sketches [laying on monochrome or colour washes]. In the evening wrote to Jaffer Khan informing him of our intention of leaving this tomorrow for Sirinagur.
21 April. Were all greatly disappointed this morning in not finding the hill Men ready to march with us – on that account were obliged to halt another day. . . . Gave the hill men some Money in the morning which induced others to come & offer their services.' (*Journal*)

The Daniells, whose jampans or carrying chairs can be seen under the tree on the left of the engraving, camped at Kotdwara at the foot of the pass leading into the mountains towards Srinagar. They appear to have been the first Europeans to follow that route.

45

44

46 47

46 'View in the Koah Nullah' (IV, *Twenty-Four Landscapes*, 15)
22 April 1789. 'Left Coadwar Gaut abt ½ af 6 and marched to Juganor – the Scenes the whole way of the most romantic kind – impassable for any animal. We all four were carried in our Jampans by four Bearers to each who seemed to take us with great ease. Saw many Villages & much cultivation on the tops of the hills as we came on.' (*Journal*)

The party followed the rocky valley of the Khoh River.

47 'Jugeanor, in the Mountains of Sirinagur' (IV, *Twenty-Four Landscapes*, 16)
22 April 1789. 'Jugeanor [Jhawanu] is a small irregular place; the zemindar, or chief landholder of the neighbourhood, like the village squires of other countries, is lodged more sumptuously than his inferiors; his mansion is tolerably built of stone, covered with slates, and consists of two stories, the upper one accommodating the chief and his family, the lower affording shelter to his cattle.'

When the Daniells arrived the villagers were reaping their wheat. The artists were interested to find that their attendants, who were Bengalis and rice-eaters, despised this food. The prejudice has persisted. In recent famines, when wheat was brought to Bengal many villagers starved rather than eat it. The Daniells' servants were also prejudiced against 'beautiful transparent water' flowing in the hills: 'their stagnant reservoirs, and even the turbid waters of the Hoogley at Calcutta, appeared to them much more inviting'.

48

48 'Near Dusa, in the Mountains of Sirinagur' (IV, *Twenty-Four Landscapes*, 18)

23 April 1789. 'Soon after we arrived at our Ground (at Dusa [Diosa]) I walked up a highish hill to look about me – saw many very grand Scenes – gathered some Yellow Raspberries – got a great quantity of them & made pudding, &c – met also with the Fir to day & many of the Fir apples – the Hills appear to be plentifully Covered with them. Met also with the Wormwood, exactly like that we get in England.' (*Journal*)

'Dusa stands on the banks of the Koah Nullah, a few miles, it is said, below its source. The forms of the mountains are, from this point, extremely bold, and all around the general effect is majestic.'

The Daniells were surprised at the 'considerable degree of population' and 'pleasant villages'. 'Security is a principal source of happiness', Thomas observed. 'The peaceful inhabitants of these hills not only enjoy a secure retreat from the perils of polished society, but a luxuriant vegetation supplies them with food, and also with gums and other articles of commerce, with which, by sale or barter, they procure from the distant plains such conveniences as their moderate system of life requires.'

49 'View on the Ram-Gunga, between Buddell & Bilkate' (IV, *Twenty-Four Landscapes*, 20)

24 April 1789. 'From the Top of the hill we descended abt 6 Koass [1 Koas = *c*. 2 miles, or 3 km] – the Path all the way to the bottom but just wide enough for one person to Walk. The Valley below of great depth, steep, & sometimes almost makes one giddy to look down. A Bangy Wollah [porter] unfortunately lost his load from the Top of one of the hills & it rolled down almost to the bottom . . .' (*Journal*)

Here, between Badel and Bilkhet, Thomas lamented that he could not record 'the visionary effect of the twilight. The beauty of the fireflies was 'still further out of the reach of imitative art': they 'illuminated every object, and diffused a magical radiance equally beautiful and surprising; it seemed in truth, to be a land of romance, and the proper residence of those fanciful beings, the fairies and genii, that appear so often in asiatic tales.'

50

51

50 'Buddell, opposite Bilkate in the Mountains of Sirinagur' (IV, *Twenty-Four Landscapes*, 19)

24 April 1789. 'Made a few Views abt Bilket &c in the course of the Day. The Villages & houses are situated & built much in the same manner as they appear in Davises Bootan Views [ill. p. 39] . . . Our tent was pitched between two small rills on a beautifull knoll.' (*Journal*)

'It being the time of harvest when this view was taken, and the corn gathered in, the mode of treading out the grain by the feet of cattle, is represented in the foreground, and also the collecting and winnowing it; all which operations are performed in the open air.'

51 'View taken between Natan & Taka Ca Munda, Sirinagur Mountains' (IV, *Twenty-Four Landscapes*, 21). *See also colour plate IX*

26 April 1789. 'From Natan [Naithana] ascended a very high mountain, from which We had a glorious view of the Snowy ones, or rather regions. The height of them far exceeded any of our expectations – they disappeared soon after the Sun had risen. On our march saw many very noble Scenes – most of the mountains cultivated from the Top to the bottom – the Cookoo the only bird we have seen or heard for many days. Met with the Pines again to day chiefly on the Northern sides of the mountains – also the Daisies in great plenty, the Dandelion, Rushes, the butter flower, St Johns Wort & the Honeysuckle a strong Woody Shrub.' (*Journal*)

52

The Daniells were deeply moved by 'the appearance of a prodigious range of still more distant mountains, proudly rising above all that we have hitherto considered as most grand and magnificent, and which, clothed in a robe of everlasting snow, seem by their etherial hue to belong to a region elevated into the clouds, and partaking of their nature; having nothing in common with terrestial forms. It would be in vain to attempt, by any description, to convey an idea of those sublime effects, which perhaps even the finest art can but faintly imitate.'

52 'Between Taka Ca Munda and Sirinagur' (IV, *Twenty-Four Landscapes*, 22)
27 April 1789. 'From Takakamurea we ascended for abt a mile, where the Snowy Mountains made a grand appearance. Un & self made a sketch of them. Began to descend very considerably to the cundar Nulla – abt 6 Koass – crossed the Nulla & ascended a Hill of abt a Mile from the top of Which you command a very fine View of Sirinagur.' (*Journal*)

'In these high situations the traveller encounters no villages; he must carry with him the means of subsistence, or perish. Taka-ca-munda is a solitary resting place; a plain stone building erected near the barren summit of one of the highest mountains, for the accommodation of benighted wanderers, or to afford an occasional shelter from the storms that frequently vex these cloud-enveloped hills.'

53

53 'View taken near the City of Sirinagur' (IV, *Twenty-Four Landscapes*, 24)
27 April 1789. 'At this place, which is a little above the city, terminated the author's rout[e] through the mountainous district of Serinagur . . . The mountains are here embellished with scattered villages, and their sides with regular horizontal stripes of cultivation, producing an effect not so agreeable to the artistical as to the philanthropic observer, who is much less interested by the beauties of form than by such unpicturesque indications of useful industry.'

From this hill the artists soon obtained a view of the city, which 'had very nearly the appearance of a Chinese Town', and the Ganges. 'We then descended abt a Mile & pitched our Tent a little to the SW of the Town very near the Ganges. Immediately after our arrival the People flocked round us in great numbers, we being the first Europeans that had ever visited Sirinagur. Soon after we pitched the Tent a shower of rain fell which made the Thermometer fall from 100 to 80 Deg [38 to 27 °C] – a change of abt 20 Degrees in the course of an hour. Abt 7 p.m. the Rajah & his Brother [ill. p. 47] paid us a Visit. A great Crowd of People came with him & our tent was so filled with them that we could hardly be heard. Made the Rajah a present of a Watch & a pair of Pistols which he seemed pleased with. He sat with us but ½ an hour. The Rajah appeared to make a great parade in Visiting us, came in a Palanquin, was attended by a Tamtoom [drum] & a kind of brazen trumpet like that of the Chinese.' (*Journal*)

54 'The Rope Bridge at Sirinagur' (IV, *Twenty-Four Landscapes*, 23)
28 April 1789. The Raja of Srinagar was in the midst of one of his recurring feuds with his brother; news was received that the latter's forces were approaching the town, and expected to arrive within two hours. 'Soon after breakfast some of the Rajahs attendants waited on us & attempted to persuade us that it was the Rajahs wish that we would cross the River (Ganges) as he thought that our present situation was not perfectly safe . . . However they were given to understand that we had not the least fear of remaining where we were, which answer seemed to surprise them. . . . After they left us Mr Sturmer Un & self went to the Bridge of Ropes over the Ganges. In consequence of the aforesaid news the inhabitants of Sirinagur were crossing the River as Quick as possible – they crowded on the Bridge so fast that we thought at times it would have broke, taking their Chesebust [luggage], Cots &c with them.' (*Journal*)

54

55

55 'View near Daramundi, in the Mountains of Serinagur' (IV, *Twenty-Four Landscapes*, 17)

3 May 1789. 'Started very early & gained the Top of a very steep hill before the Sun had much power. . . . Have scarcely seen a Rock of any other kind than Black & White marble the whole march. Found the Raspberries in great plenty to day – met also with the Cherry a number of which Un gathered & proposes taking the Stones to Boglipore [Bhagalpur] for S Davis.' (*Journal*)

'The figures . . . represent the Highland merchants on their way from the plains where they have been bartering the produce of their hills for salt, copper vessels, linen, and other wares, which they convey not in packs, like our pedestrian traders, but in baskets closely fitted and secured to their backs; relieving themselves occasionally from the incumbent weight by the application of a short staff, carried by each traveller for that purpose, to the bottom of the basket, while he takes his standing rest. In this manner these indefatigable creatures, that seem no larger than ants, compared with the stupendous heights they have to traverse, pursue their laborious journey.'

The return May 1789 to November 1791

THE DANIELLS NOW set off on their return journey. They planned to spend the next two months travelling down to Lucknow so that they would reach the city before the rains broke. Again the country was little known to the British and as yet unadministered by them. On 8 May they left Najibabad with its fine mosque and tomb of the Rohilla chief, Najib-ud-Daula. It was now very hot and the 20-mile (32-kilometre) march to Nagina was most unpleasant, a high wind blowing up the dust. At Nagina they found their perambulator had broken and there seemed no chance of repairing it before reaching Rampur. On 11 May they reached Kashipur, where they camped in a mango grove and spent a day colouring their drawings. They were delighted to get news that the Srinagar Raja had made a stand: the Kumaon forces 'were so warmly pelted with stones from the top of the hill that they fled in great confusion. About 200 men were killed.' At Rampur, the capital of the Rohilla country, the ruler Faizullah Khan called upon them and supplied their servants with flour, cooking oil and salt. The next day, 14 May, they returned his call and spent a very pleasant hour discussing 'the customs and manners of the English' with him. He sent them a 'cooked dinner & supper in the Moorman's stile' as well as a guard of twenty-four sepoys. They found little to draw at Rampur so they stayed in their tents and showed their drawings to Faizullah Khan's *munshi*, who was 'much struck with them'. The next day the party made an expedition to Moradabad while the perambulator was being repaired. They then left Rampur and made a detour to Pilibhit (*no.* 56, *X*) before travelling through Dhakia and Bisauli to the Ganges, which they probably reached at Kachhla. Here they hired a boat and sailed down to Kanauj, where they were delighted by the ruins of the once famous city (*nos.* 57, 58, *XI*). Leaving the boat at Cawnpore they went by land to Lucknow, where they arrived early in July.

Here they were to remain throughout the rains until about mid-October. They were given generous hospitality by Colonel Claud Martin (1735–1800), whom they had met in Calcutta. This French officer was in the service of Asaf-ud-Daula, Nawab of Oudh (ruled 1775–97), whose capital was at Lucknow. Oudh was in theory an independent Indian state, although the Nawab's power had been severely curtailed by a treaty with the British which rendered it in practice a protectorate. Martin was a trusted adviser of Asaf-ud-Daula and superintendent of his arsenal. He possessed vast estates, was extremely rich and had cultured interests that were both European and Indian, collecting *objets d'art*, books and manuscripts as well as paintings, drawings and prints. He patronized Indian artists and any British painters who visited Lucknow, such as Zoffany, during whose various visits between 1784 and 1788 he had acquired a large number of works. He had adjusted himself to Indian life and had an Indian 'wife' or *bibi*. When the Daniells visited him he was living in a fine house, the Farad Baksh, on the River Gumti, surrounded by all his collections. While staying with him the artists were therefore introduced to a very different India from the one they had experienced in Calcutta. They met not only the British Resident and the British community but also Indian gentry. They even accompanied Martin to the Nawab's court, where they breakfasted and watched elephant fights and nautches.

During their stay Thomas and William Daniell were employed by Martin in a number of ways. Thomas was asked to 'finish' some of Zoffany's sketches. On 20 July William noted in his diary, 'Looked over several of Zoffany's sketches this morning – the Col. put many out, which my Un. [Uncle] means to put backgrounds to.' The next day, 'Un. put a background to a faquiere [fakir] of Zoffany's this morning. Got down the four large Pictures that hung up in the hall of the Col.'s Bungalow & began to clean and repair them.' On 27 July Thomas was finishing a slight sketch of Zoffany's made near Najafgarh, a place where Martin had a small bungalow. Some weeks later he 'laid in a pillow or two' behind Prince Jawan Bakht, the son of the Mughal Emperor, who had been portrayed by Zoffany in 1784. At the same time the artists were probably availing of the break from travelling and camping to arrange their drawings and work up unfinished sketches of their own. They made a few expeditions to neighbouring places of interest – Faizabad (*no.* 59), the capital of Asaf-ud-Daula's father, Shuja-ud-Daula, and Ayodhya, one of the seven sacred Hindu

This watercolour of Kanauj by William Daniell, inscribed '1790', which must have been based on a pencil or wash drawing made in June 1789, illustrates the manner in which an aquatint evolved. A long time often elapsed between the making of a sketch on the spot and the second stage of a full watercolour. A comparison of this drawing with the final print (*no.* 58) shows how changes were made yet again: figures and foliage were added to enliven the picture, while other figures were removed from the arches to contribute to the mood of empty desolation that pervaded the ruins. (Private collection)

The circle of Colonel Claud Martin in Lucknow, *c.*1787. Zoffany shows himself in the centre, seated at his easel in the house of Colonel Antoine Polier. Polier, a collector of Indian manuscripts and miniatures, is seated on the left giving orders to his servants, while on the right Colonel Martin, paint brushes in hand, shows to the Company's Paymaster, John Wombwell, a watercolour he has painted of his own house, the Farad Baksh – where the Daniells were to stay. (Victoria Memorial, Calcutta)

cities where William Hodges had taken several views. William commented acidly, 'Could not find the view of one of the Ghats which Hodges has made an Aquatinta print of, there not being one of them like what he has represented.'

In spite of the pleasant time they spent in Lucknow, the Daniells were disappointed at the lack of patronage from the Nawab. As soon as they arrived, Martin had taken the artists to visit him and the next day the Nawab breakfasted at Martin's house and looked at their drawings. Martin showed him a set of Thomas Daniell's *Views of Calcutta* and the Nawab expressed a wish to have a similar set made for him of Lucknow. During August therefore the Daniells made drawings of the city (*nos. 60–62, XII*) and also experimented with engraving on copper and iron plates. They must have been most disappointed when on 7 September the Nawab again breakfasted with Martin and, after looking at this material, went away without giving them any order. Asaf-ud-Daula in fact had little interest in European art. He had already commissioned work from Zoffany, Ozias Humphry and Charles Smith and he was becoming tired of visits from British artists. Portraits were a form of flattery but landscapes had little appeal. He far preferred the colourful miniatures made by indigenous local artists. Nevertheless, through the hospitality of Colonel Martin Lucknow must have been a highly stimulating episode in the artists' journey across Northern India. After months of travelling they passed the rainy season in comfort and were able to organize their large stock of paintings and drawings.

About the middle of October, the Daniells set off once more on their travels. William does not recommence his diary until 22 October, by which time he and his uncle had reached Dalmau on the Ganges, some 60 or so miles (about 100 kilometres) below Cawnpore. It is probable that they travelled back from Lucknow to Cawnpore overland and then hired a boat to retrace the route by which they had earlier gone up-country. The cold weather now stretched ahead. There was less need to hurry as long as they reached Bhagalpur, where they were going to stay with Samuel Davis, by the next hot weather. They could spend more time at places such as Allahabad, Chunar and Benares through which they had been forced to hurry on their way upstream. They could also make a number of detours to other places about which they had heard interesting reports.

During the early part of the journey down the river the artists experienced various difficulties with the boat. They drew Dalmau fort on 22 October while they were waiting for the anchor of their pinnace to be repaired. Then the boat lodged on sandbanks. However they made drawings at Nobusta and Kara (*no. 63*). By 30 October they had reached Allahabad. They had passed the city rapidly on the way up-country so they now stopped and spent about a week drawing the fort with its great gateways and fine pavilions (*no. 64*). They also visited the mausoleum of Prince Khusrau, the eldest son of the Emperor Jahangir, in a garden to the west of the city (*nos. 65–68, XIII*). They were fortunate to be at Allahabad during an eclipse of the moon, when crowds of Hindus congregated at the sacred confluence of the Ganges and Jumna Rivers.

This nineteenth-century photograph of the Atala Mosque at Jaunpur confirms both the accuracy of the Daniells' view (*no. 73*) and the rightness of Hodges' emotional reaction in his aquatint, *opposite*. (India Office Library and Records, London)

They continued down the Ganges past Mirzapur to Chunargarh, where they stopped for four days (*nos. 69, 70*). This was an obvious place to halt as there was an army cantonment and a number of British residents to give them hospitality. The artists were also keen to draw the entrance gateway to the mosque which Hodges had published. They then moved on to Benares to draw the many ghats and buildings which they had failed to record on the journey upriver. From 17 November they worked away for about a week (*nos. 71, 72*), in the course of which they witnessed an eclipse of the sun. Once again they were critical of Hodges: one of his views near Benares was 'so very unlike that one would imagine he had taken it under full sail'. From Benares they decided to make a detour to Jaunpur, for Hodges had drawn various buildings in that city also and they were not to be outdone. Jaunpur, once known as the 'Shiraz of India', had been the capital of an independent Muslim kingdom until the Mughal Emperor Akbar captured it in 1559. It abounded in splendid buildings, especially the fort, the bridge, the Jami Mosque, the Lal Darwaza Mosque and above all the Atala Mosque with its sturdy entrance (*no. 73*). When the artists were ready to leave on 13 December the boat they were expecting had not arrived, and they were forced to spend a dreary night under the lee of a Hindu building, comforting themselves as well as they could 'with a Piece of Bread & a little Brandy & Water'. By 16 December they were back at Sikraul, the civil station on the outskirts of Benares. Here Thomas showed his drawings to the British Resident, James Grant, and to Captain Cullen. They went on to Benares hoping to make a general view of the city but unfortunately a spell of rain lasting three or four days forced them to stay in their tent. On the way back to Sikraul, however, they stopped to buy some sturdy country-bred ponies, as they

Aquatints by William Hodges from his *Select Views*.

'A View of a Mosque at Chunar Gur' (no. 19, published 20 December 1786) provides a vivid contrast to Thomas Daniell's engraving (*no. 69*): the viewpoints are different, and where Daniell emphasized the architectural ornament, Hodges saw the gateway as part of a picturesque composition, merely suggesting the ornament by means of impressionistic strokes.

'A View of a Musjd, i.e. Tomb at Jionpoor' (no. 13, published 15 September 1786). Through the boldly foreshortened perspective – a favourite device – Hodges conveys the overwhelming force of the architecture of the Atala Mosque. But again, he provides little detail for an architect in England.

were now planning another rigorous tour in the footsteps of William Hodges.

This trek had been stimulated by Hodges' engravings of the hill-forts situated in the jungly terrain south of Chunargarh. His drawings had resulted from a traumatic experience in Benares in August 1781 when he had accompanied Warren Hastings to the city with the hope of coming to some agreement with the Raja, Chet Singh. Finding the Raja truculent, Hastings put him under house-arrest at Shivala Ghat on grounds of 'disaffection and infidelity'. The next day, the Raja's men rose up against the British troops. Three companies of sepoys and their British officers were killed; Chet Singh escaped across the river to Ramnagar (*no. 23*). Hastings was left with only a small force. He sent for reinforcements, but on their arrival these were attacked by the Raja as they made their way through the narrow alleys to the palace and were forced to retreat. Hastings had no alternative but to leave Benares hurriedly on the evening of 20 August. He and his party, which included Hodges, marched throughout the night and arrived at Chunargarh next morning. For Hodges this was an unforgettable experience. In mid-September an offensive against the Raja began and his three forts were eventually all captured. He himself escaped to Central India. Hodges was now able to return at the end of the month to Benares, from where he made excursions to the various forts where the engagements had taken place. He received a number of commissions for oil paintings of the forts from the officers involved in their capture.

When the Daniells started on their tour of the area, almost ten years had elapsed since these events had taken place. The forts had lost their topical interest for the British but Thomas Daniell was clearly attracted by the wildness of the surrounding country, the rocky hills and picturesque views. He had not as yet seen country of this type. Not to be outdone by Hodges, he was to explore the area thoroughly and later work up a number of oils. He did not bother, however, to publish views of the forts. The two artists began the tour by leaving Benares on 29 December for Chunargarh, where they stayed with a merchant friend, Benjamin D'Aguilar. On New Year's Day 1790 they set off about 7 o'clock and marched south and then south-west, covering about 10 miles (16 kilometres) to Saktisgarh, where the hills dropped sharply to the plains. They spent the next day drawing the waterfalls there – 'upon the Whole the most romantic place we have met with in our travels. Were told there were a number of Tygers & Wolves near the place but saw neither', wrote William. On 3 January they struck east, skirting the hills and following the Barhi River to Pattihata ('Pateta') where Hodges had drawn the fort. The next day they left at noon and swung south-east to Latifpur, the second of Chet Singh's forts. It still appeared strong, although many of the beams in the rooms had been taken away and the inside was filled with jungle inhabited by langur monkeys. Then they moved south to Lohra ('Lahore'), where a battle had been fought between Chet Singh and the British, but they found it a very 'miserable place'. From Lohra they travelled east to Semariea ('Simoriah') and then due south to Mau at the foot of the Bijaigarh range.

Here they were in jungly country which was eminently suitable for sketching. They could not wait: immediately on arriving at Mau on 7 January they 'got one of the Company's Seapoys to procure a guide or two' to the Bijaigarh fort, which cost them 'about an hour ascending'. This was the third of Chet Singh's forts and Hodges had painted it several times. The hills were steep and rocky and the next day was spent in climbing around so as to find good views. They made one sketch from a hill to the south 'where the British placed 2 cannon at the time of the Cannonading'. In spite of discouragement from the guides, they scrambled down to the plain on the west side of the fort and 'were well repaid for our trouble by the many Views we were presented with afterward'. Most of the next day passed 'abt the Gate & bridge near Mow [Mau]. Abt 1 mile [1·5 kilometres] below the bridge the bed of the River being very rocky the Water falls over abt 40 ft [12 metres]. On our return from the fall perceived very plainly the footstep of a Tiger that had come to the River to Drink.'

Thomas and William Daniell viewing Bijaigarh from the south-west (detail of a watercolour by William, 8 January 1790). Thomas is seated with a drawing board on his knee, shaded by an awning; William is peering through a telescope at the fort, his drawing board (and a dog) nearby. (P & O Steam Navigation Company Collection)

On 11 January they travelled west for about 5 miles (8 kilometres) to Pokhraur Ghat ('Eckpouah Ghat'). The first part of the journey was through 'jungle & pleasant Wood. Within ½ a Mile [800 metres] before we descended to the Gaut a very fine Scene presented itself, a deep dell before us richly wooded, the nulla from Bidze Gur running thro' it – on the Right bold picturesque rocks, on the left gently sloping hills, the distance terminating with the valley through which the Son runs. Agouri [Agori] appeared in View over the hills to the left.' At the ghat they found their horses had to make their way down an almost perpendicular rock about 12 or 14 feet (4 metres) high. The whole area around Bijaigarh is still difficult for travellers today. In 1974 when the District Officer at Benares was approached concerning an expedition to this spot he declared it 'impossible'.

The Daniells continued south to Markundi ('Mocoonru'). They were now on easier ground and on 12 January they arrived a Mitapur on the Son River opposite Agori. A 'person from the Fort' crossed the river and informed them that the Raja was absent for a few days but that every attention would be paid

A drawing of the temple of Mandesvara, typical of the rapid sketches made on the spot in pencil and wash which the Daniells later worked up into watercolours and finally engraved (*no. 76*). (Spink & Son Ltd)

to them. They were taken over in a 'small flat bottom Canoe' – their horses and bullocks swimming after them – and were shown over the fort. Several days were spent at Agori where the artists made a drawing of the temples amongst banyan trees (*no. 74, XIV*). They were very glad to receive some bread and fresh vegetables from Mr D'Aguilar, their friend at Chunar, whose coolie had taken five days to reach them. A young black monkey was caught while they were there.

From Agori they set off in a north-eastery direction skirting the hills. William's diary misses out a few days at this point but on 19 January they reached Bagheta Ghat ('Burghutta Gaut') and managed to get their horses down the bad road to Ramgarh (*no. 75*). Here they stayed for two or three days as they heard there were a number of ruined temples in the neighbourhood. Outstanding among these was the temple of Mandesvara, which lay buried under debris and overgrown to the roof with bushes and trees (*nos. 76, 77*): they crawled inside and found the temple perfect with a fine Shiva lingam. In the vicinity were several other temples with sculpture lying around. They moved on to Bhabua through Chainpur where they were attracted by the Muslim *idgah* surrounded by a wall with rich embellishments (*no. 78*).

On 25 January they left Bhabua and set out for the fort of Shergarh, travelling via Bagwanpur and Bahuri ('Boohoolee') to Durgauti ('Duurgooty'). They were passing through wild jungle, where they received news of a tiger and one of the servants saw four large bears. They reached Shergarh on 28 January and spent the next day making drawings of the fort and the rocky landscape – 'one of the boldest Crags we have met with – Un. says he never saw any in Yorkshire equal it.' From Shergarh they continued north-east to Karma and east to Ugahni ('Uganee'). They then struck south up into the hills to Bhurkura ('Bhoorcoon-

The Daniells picknicking at the hot springs of Sitakund with Samuel Davis, who is smoking a hookah. Detail of a wash drawing by Davis, 1790. (Victoria Memorial, Calcutta)

Samuel Davis's house at Bhagalpur, drawn by himself and inscribed 'my bungalow'. Their stay in this comfortable house in October 1788 and again for nearly a year in 1790–91 must have given the Daniells the greatest relief after the strain of constant travelling. (Victoria Memorial, Calcutta)

dah'), where on 30 January they visited a cave near the Goptha River ('Gooput Benares').

At this point William's diary ends, but from dated drawings it is possible to reconstruct the remainder of their travels until their return to Calcutta in the autumn of 1791. From the Shergarh area they dropped down to the plains and took the easy road to Sasaram. They must have been exhausted from their rigorous tour through the hills and jungles of eastern Uttar Pradesh and western Bihar. They rested some time at Sasaram, drawing Sher Shah's mausoleum which Hodges had visited and illustrated in his *Dissertation on the prototypes of architecture, Hindoo, Moorish and Gothic* (1787). In February they set out for the great Mughal fort of Rohtasgarh, travelling by the plain which skirted the Son River. On the way they stopped to draw the waterfalls near Tarachandi known as Dhuan Kund ('Dhuah Koonde'), the Pool of Smoke (*no. 79, XV*). They then ascended to the fort by the road from Akbarpur. It is clear from the many drawings and engravings of the fort and its surroundings (*nos. 80–83, XVI*) that they delighted in this splendid monument and its high, romantic setting.

Having finished their work they made their way back by the same route to Dehri where they crossed the Son and continued to the holy city of Gaya by way of Deo and Madanpur. In both these places they drew Hindu temples (*nos. 84–86*) and at Gaya (*no. 87, XVII*) they saw the famous shrines and the sacred banyan tree (*no. 88*). They also explored the Barabar Caves – the 'Marabar Caves' of E. M. Forster's *A Passage to India*, where Miss Quested had her terrifying experience. Continuing north through Hilsa to Patna, they visited once more the mausoleum of Makhdam Shah Daulat at Maner (*no. 22*). From Patna they almost certainly travelled by boat to Bhagalpur, where they were to stay for more than a year with Samuel Davis.

It was now the hot weather of 1790 and the rains would soon break. The artists had had enough of constant travelling and must have been thankful for the quiet and comfort of their old friend's house. From time to time they made short expeditions up and down the river and to neighbouring places of interest with Davis. A river expedition was probably made to the Fakir's Rock at Sultanganj (*nos. 89, 90, XVIII*) and they picknicked at the hot springs of Sitakund near Monghyr. Thomas thought the waters here were better than those of Bath. But for most of the time they were working hard. They now had a vast store of drawings; a number of the more attractive subjects had already

Detail of a watercolour by Samuel Davis of the Kotwali Gate at Gaur, 1791. It is possibly Thomas Daniell who is sketching, accompanied by a Bengal sepoy with 'sundial' turban, an orderly, a fan-bearer, and a dog. (Private collection)

been worked up into full watercolours, but at the moment they were concerned with producing a large number of oil paintings ready for sale on their return to Calcutta. They needed to raise money for yet another tour and the obvious method was a lottery, one of the most popular ways of obtaining money for almost any purpose, such as the building of a church or a town hall, the founding of a school or the selling of an indigo factory. The cost of tickets varied according to the value of the prizes and could range from fifteen to several hundred rupees. In the quiet of Bhagalpur, away from the social life of Calcutta, the Daniells were able to work up over a hundred oil paintings of various sizes for this crucial sale.

Towards the end of the rains in 1791 they set off for Calcutta, probably accompanied by Samuel Davis. Disaster almost overtook them near Rajmahal, where their baggage boat capsized and they lost all their goods apart from their drawings and paintings which they had kept with them. On the way back they stopped at Gaur, about 150 miles (240 kilometres) up the river from Calcutta. This ancient city had declined after the outbreak of plague in 1575 and the fine city walls and gateways, palaces, mosques and tombs were rapidly disappearing under the encroaching jungle. It provided a number of attractive subjects (*nos. 91, 92*), including the Dakhil and Kotwali gates. Hodges had stopped there, so the site could not be missed.

The artists probably arrived back in Calcutta in November 1791, as William Baillie in a letter of 23 November notes that 'Mr Thomas Daniell returned to Calcutta . . . with a collection of about 150 pictures.' A lottery was announced by the *Calcutta Gazette* on 5 January 1792 and the pictures were displayed in the Old Harmonic Tavern. The draw took place on 1 March with apparently satisfactory results, although William complained in a letter to his mother that people were 'more ready to admire Uncle's paintings than buy them'. In the meantime the two artists busied themselves making additional drawings of the city, which included fresh views of the Esplanade, the Council House, Writers' Buildings and the Chitpore Bazaar with its little temple (*nos. 93–95, 97*).

xii (62)

xiii (65) >

XIV (74)

< XVII (87)

XVIII (89)

56

56 'Gate of a Mosque built by Hafiz Ramut, Pillibeat' (III, *Oriental Scenery*, 10). *See also colour plate X*
17 May 1789. 'The Mosque to which this gate belongs, is a handsome edifice richly ornamented ... much in the style of the modern buildings of the same class at Delhi.'

The builder of the mosque, Hafiz Rahmat Khan, a Rohilla Afghan, had been killed in 1774 after reneging on a pact with the Nawab of Oudh to fight the much-feared Marathas. Faizullah Khan, whom the Daniells met, was his great-nephew.

In the road is a canopied bullock carriage. The soldier in the foreground has the curling-toed shoes worn by Muslims.

57 'Cannoge on the River Ganges' (IV, *Twenty-Four Landscapes*, 12)
May 1789. Kanauj, a very ancient site, had once been a flourishing city: Fanny Parks believed that it had contained 'thirty thousand shops, in which betel-nut was sold; and sixty thousand bands of musicians and singers, who paid a tax to Government'. Thomas Daniell was moved to brood: 'It is impossible to look at these miserable remnants of the great city of Cannoge without the most melancholy sensations, and the strongest conviction of the instability of man's proudest works. ... The plains of India indeed present to mankind many a sad proof of the uncertainty of human glory.'

57

58 'Ruins at Cannouge' (III, *Oriental Scenery*, 7). *See also colour plate XI*

May 1789. The Daniells were clearly impressed by the great mosque, seen on the left, which had been built in 1406 by Ibrahim Shah of Jaunpur, and guessed correctly that old stonework had been re-used in it. It stands, Thomas writes, 'on the site of a Hindoo temple, and probably much of the ancient materials have been again brought into use by the Mahomedans, (a frequent practice with them, after mutilating every ornament that had any reference to the Hindoo mythology) the pillars, and some other parts, being evidently Hindoo.'

59 'Gate of the Loll-Baug at Fyzabad' (III, *Oriental Scenery*, 3)

11–12 July 1789. Faizabad had been the capital of Oudh under Shuja-ud-Daula (ruled 1754–75), and though his son had moved the capital back to Lucknow (see *no. 60*) it was still an impressive city. It had a great market which was entered through a three-arched gateway, and Shuja's palace was described by Hodges in 1782 as 'a vast building . . . having several areas or courts, and many separate buildings in them'. Shuja had also laid out three gardens, one of them the Lal Bagh (Red Garden), the gate of which is seen here.

'Loll Bhaug', writes Thomas Daniell, 'is the name given to a garden made by Nawaub Sujah al Dowla. The gate is elegantly designed, and highly enriched with ornaments: its principal apartment is over the entrance, to which are attached two balconies; the roof is flat and terraced. The surrounding wall is of stone stuccoed, and at the angles are pavilions of an octagonal form. This garden is at a considerable distance from the the palace, a circumstance not unusual with the opulent of India; places of this description, which may be truly called pleasure gardens, are generally large, intersected by straight paved walks, bordered with shrubs and flowers, and contain a variety of the most delicate fruits; they are embellished with several very elegant pavilions, where the master occasionally seats himself to enjoy his Hooka, singing, dancing, etc. to which may also be added the exercise of swinging, whirling in the Hindola, and various other similar amusements, with which the Indians are much delighted.'

60 'Palace of Nawaub Suja Dowla, at Lucnow' (III, *Oriental Scenery*, 16)

July–October 1789. The Nawabs of Oudh were nominally governors of a large province of the Mughal Empire, but as Mughal power declined they became virtually independent. Oudh was one of the most fertile areas of Upper India and its capital, Lucknow, became a flourishing and beautiful city. Nawab Shuja-ud-Daula spent the first eleven years of his reign at Lucknow and built himself a palace there. In 1764, however, he was defeated at the battle of Buxar, with the result that Oudh lost some of its territory to the British and Shuja moved his capital to a more central position at Faizabad (*no. 59*). After his death, his son, Asaf-ud-Daula, returned to Lucknow and started to rebuild the city on a grandiose scale. It was during this period that the Daniells arrived there.

The picture shows the palace built by Shuja some time between 1754 and 1764. On the right, beside the building with a pyramidal roof, is the Panch Mahal gateway (*no. 62*).

58

59

60

61

61 'Lucnow taken from the Opposite Bank of the River Goomty' (III, *Oriental Scenery*, 17)
July–October 1789. This aquatint continues the panorama of the river bank begun in *no. 60*. 'Part of the palace of Nawaub Sujah ul Dowla is seen on the left, the mosque appears highly elevated, and the new Palace of the present Nawaub Asoph ul Dowla, is seen along the water's edge, extending a considerable way up the river.'

The city with its shining white buildings along the Gumti River must have presented a noble appearance. As the *Oriental Annual* (1835) noted, 'It is astonishing to what a degree of perfection the natives of India carry out the art of stuccoing . . . producing an effect so near to that of white marble, that it often requires a close scrutiny to detect the imitation.'

62

62 'The Punj Mahalla Gate, Lucnow' (III, *Oriental Scenery*, 5). *See also colour plate XII*

July–October 1789. 'The plainness and simplicity of this edifice is more striking than the richness of its decorations; a circumstances seldom occurring in gateways belonging to Mahomedan princes. This gate leads to a palace erected by Nawaub Sujah ul Dowla' (*nos. 60, 61*).

The fish emblem of the Nawabs of Oudh can be seen in the plasterwork on the gate, which shows the solid simple architecture of Shuja-ud-Daula's reign that was being replaced by his son's ornate white stucco buildings. The entrance is approached by a ramp allowing elephants easy access to the inner courtyard.

63

63 'View from the Ruins of the Fort of Currah, on the River Ganges' (III, *Oriental Scenery*, 21)

25 October 1789. With the rains over the artists set out on their return journey by river. Once again they were attracted by the scenery near Kara. 'What appears in this view was formerly part of a gateway. From this spot the view down the river Ganges has a good effect, the banks are well clothed with Mango topes, or groves, richly interspersed with buildings, boats, etc.'

Thomas Daniell delighted in 'singular' forms, which were valued in the new aesthetic approach to landscape, and this scene was clearly chosen because of the interesting shape of the ruin.

64 'Part of the Palace in the Fort of Allahabad' (I, *Oriental Scenery*, 8)

6 November 1789. 'Spent the day in the fort, chiefly employed in making correct drawings of the Ornaments in the Buildings which we have made Views of. Ther. this morning 64 [18°C].' (*Journal*)

Today little of architectural interest remains within Akbar's fort (see *no. 24*), but one of the few surviving buildings is this elegant marble *baradari* or pavilion surrounded by pillars. The terraced roof has a perforated parapet and is surmounted by kiosks with latticed screens. It was already damaged when the Daniells saw it. 'In the centre of the terrace, on the top of the building', Thomas notes, 'stood a turret of white marble, very elegantly finished, which was taken down by order of the nabob of Oud, and sent to Lucknow, . . . with the intention, it is said, to be again erected in that city: a circumstance much to be lamented.'

Humphry Repton copied these kiosks when designing a pheasantry for the Royal Pavilion at Brighton in 1806.

65 'The Entrance to the Mausoleums in Sultan Khusero's Garden, near Allahabad' (III, *Oriental Scenery*, 8). *See also colour plate XIII*

66 'Mausoleum of Sultan Chusero, near Allahabad' (I, *Oriental Scenery*, 17)

c. 7 November 1789. The Khusrau Bagh (garden) outside Allahabad was originally built by a pupil of the imperial architect Aqa Riza as a pleasure resort for Prince Salim, Akbar's son, later the Emperor Jahangir (ruled 1605–27). After some time the Prince made it over to his son Khusrau, but when the latter rebelled against him in 1606 he imprisoned him there. Khusrau was eventually handed over to his step-brother, later Shah Jahan; in 1622 he was murdered by a hired assassin and his body taken to the Khusrau Bagh for burial.

The garden is entered by a gate 60 feet (18 m) high and 46 feet (14 m) deep. 'This gate is the principal entrance to the garden in which Sultan Khusero, his mother the Ranee, and his brother Sultaun Purveiz, are interred. Though a massy structure, it has by no means a heavy effect; and though it formerly may have appeared

66

with more splendour, having been painted with different colours, that surface is fortunately now nearly washed off. The upper part towards the garden is much decayed.'

The tomb of Prince Khusrau (*no. 66*) 'is situated amidst trees of considerable magnitude in a handsome garden, laid out in the Hindoostan taste, with paved walks, avenues, and fountains. The Mausoleum is built of freestone upon a paved terrace, and the whole has a grand effect.' The interior is ornamented with Persian couplets and paintings of trees and flowers which have now faded.

This garden, with its tombs, was frequently visited by the British on their way up and down the Ganges. In 1844 Fanny Parks was invited 'to spend the day at Sultan Khusrau's garden, to which place a tent had been sent, which was pitched under the fine tamarind trees in a most picturesque place.' The first and largest tomb, she noted, is that of Sultan Khusrau, 'and within it is deposited a beautifully illuminated kuran, which the darogah [head constable] showed us with great pride'.

65

67

67 'Mausoleum of the Ranee, Wife of the Emperor Jehangire, near Allahabad' (III, *Oriental Scenery*, 4)

c. 7 November 1789. 'This lady was an Hindoo princess, although married to a Mahomedan prince, and was called the Ranee, conformably to the Hindoo usage; her Mausoleum is in the large garden near Allahabad, where are the tombs also of several of the Mogul family [see *nos. 65, 66*]. It has a grand effect from the simplicity of its plan, is executed with great care, and as a Mahomedan edifice, is very remarkable in being without pointed arches of any kind. A large fountain is attached to it. Mangoe and other umbrageous trees surround the buildings.'

Jahangir's wife, Maryam-uz-Zamari, the mother of Prince Khusrau, was the daughter of Raja Bharmal of Amber (now Jaipur) in Rajasthan.

68

68 'Mausoleum of Sultan Purveiz, near Allahabad' (I, *Oriental Scenery*, 22)

c. 7 November 1789. 'The remains of Sultan Purveiz, the son of the Emperor Jehangire, were here deposited about the year 1626. The simplicity of the general design of this Mausoleum, with its judicious and well-executed decorations, rank it among the most correct examples of Indian architecture. By time and neglect, however, this building is much impaired. The dome was originally covered with glazed tiles, so formed and disposed, as to produce a very rich effect, and of which there are many beautiful examples still remaining at Agra and Delhi. This Mausoleum is in the same garden near to that of his brother Sultan Chusero.' (*no. 66*)

Thomas Daniell had been told that this was the tomb of Parviz, the brother of Khusrau. That is now thought to be unlikely, but its identification is still uncertain.

The mausoleum appears to have been the source of the design for 'A Villa in the Eastern Style' published in 1805 by Robert Lugar.

69

70

71

69 'Gate leading to a Musjed, at Chunar Ghur' (I, *Oriental Scenery*, 24)
70 'Mausoleum of Kausim Solemanee, at Chunar Gur' (III, *Oriental Scenery*, 23)

c.13–16 November 1789. Chunargarh was a well-known landmark on the journey up and down the Ganges and many of the British stopped to explore the various historic buildings there. By the Daniells' time the old Mughal fort on the cliff-top was used by the British as a European invalid station for wounded and sick soldiers.

'The effect of this gate, at a distance, is grand, from the bold projection of its superior parts; and its ornaments, though numerous, are applied with so much art and discretion, as to form the happiest union of beauty and grandeur.'

Hodges had published a print of this seventeenth-century mosque gateway (*no. 69*) in his *Select Views* (ill. p. 99) and there is little doubt that Thomas made his engraving to show how superior his work was to that of the rival artist. While Hodges had used large trees to frame the gateway seen from the front, Thomas Daniell reduced the trees and concentrated on the detailed recording of the architecture with the gateway seen at an angle. The different attitudes of the two men to landscape painting are clearly represented by their contrasting aquatints. But although Hodges did not show details, he was well aware of them. The building reminded him of Gothic architecture: 'In this all the minor ornaments are the same – the lozenge squares filled with roses, the ornaments in the spandrels of the arches, the little pannelling, and their mouldings, so that a person would almost be led to think that artists had arrived from the same school at the same time, to erect similar buildings at the extremity of India and of Europe.'

'The Mausoleum', Thomas Daniell writes of *no. 70*, 'is of modern workmanship, and in tolerably good repair; it is built of freestone, and in many parts covered with stucco. The outer wall which surrounds the area, is very curiously ornamented on the top with lattice-work, cut in stone with the greatest exactness, and the design varying in almost every pannel.'

71 'Dusasumade Gaut, at Bernares, on the Ganges' (I, *Oriental Scenery*, 16)
c.17–25 November 1789. The Dasasamadhi Ghat, where Brahma was said to have sacrificed ten horses, is one of the five most celebrated places of pilgrimage in Benares and the main approach to the river.

Lady Nugent, as she sailed past on 22 August 1812, gave an enthusiastic description of Benares in her journal: 'The city is situated on a high semicircular bank and reaches down to the water's edge. Mosques, pagodas, temples, houses of different sorts – long flights of steps, leading to places of worship – the river, magnificently extended . . . nothing can be more striking and imposing than the first view of Benares. All the buildings are of stone, and seem likely to stand the ravages of time; as they all appear to be in good repair, and those down close to the Ganges have hitherto resisted the powerful attacks of the gigantic river, without the smallest injury. The tridents and crescents on the tops of the different Hindoo and Mussulman temples, are all of brass, or gilt and in the sun make a most magnificent appearance. The gardens look very pretty, mixed with different buildings, and large trees hanging over their walls. The multitudes of people, bathing or praying give a most indescribable effect.'

72 'The Baolee at Ramnagur' (III, *Oriental Scenery*, 20)
c.17–25 November 1789. 'This spacious Baolee is a public bath of modern workmanship, built of freestone by Rajah Cheyt Sing [ruled 1770–81] near his palace at Ramnagur on the river Ganges; it is in a mixed style of architecture in which the Mahomedan evidently prevails.' For Chet Singh's palace-fort, see *no. 23*.

73 'A Mosque at Juanpore' (III, *Oriental Scenery*, 9)
26 November 1789. 'Arrived at Jaunpore at 6 AM dist. from Benares 18 Koass. Breakfasted in the Patilla Boat that was sent from Benares some days ago & which arrived at Jaunpore Yesterday – Abt 9 o C. set out & visited the Fort, Mosques, & other buildings of note.
2 December. Spent the morning at the Atouleah Kan Musjid. Un. made a sketch of the East Gate.
3 December. Employed the whole Day at the Atouleah Kan Musjid. It is said that the Musjid cost 70 Lacks of Rupees Buildg which is as much as the Tage Mahl cost.' (*Journal*)

Jaunpur was the capital of an independent Muslim kingdom until the Mughal Emperor Akbar captured it in 1559. The Atala Mosque, completed in 1408, was built on the site of an old Hindu temple dedicated to Atala Devi. It is, Thomas Daniell comments, 'in a very singular, as well as ancient, style of building. The Minars are united by the lofty pointed arch, over which on the inside there is a terraced platform for the convenience of the crier to walk when engaged in calling the Mussulmen to prayers.'

William Hodges had drawn the same view of the mosque but in a strongly contrasting style (see pp. 98–99): as at Chunargarh (*no. 69*), his view is picturesque rather than documentary.

73

74 'Hindoo Temples at Agouree, on the River Soane, Bahar' (I, *Oriental Scenery*, 19). *See also colour plate XIV*

12 January 1790. 'On our arrival at Agouree a person from the Fort crossed the river (Soane) & paid us the usual Complts &c – informed us that the Rajah was absent for some days, but that every attention should be paid us during our stay at Agouree. We crossed in a small flat bottom Canoe, & were shown part of the fort by the person before mentioned.' (*Journal*)

Agori, on the River Son, 'is a place of worship of the greatest antiquity, which is obvious from the fragments of sculptured idols frequently to be met with there. The village at present is not very considerable.'

This is one of Thomas Daniell's most satisfying records of Hindu temple architecture in North India. The slim towers intermingle with the drooping roots of the great banyan tree to form a delightful composition.

74

75 'Ramgur' (IV, *Twenty-Four Landscapes*, 10)
19 January 1790. 'The bad road was of great continuance, however we got our horses down very well without any accident – arrived at Ramgur abt 12 o C.' (*Journal*)

'Ramgur [Ramgarh], or Rampoor, in the district of Benares, is an Hindoo village, delightfully situated in a valley sheltered by hills, richly clothed with woods. From the numerous fragments of ancient buildings that lay scattered about this village and its neighbourhood, it is evident that Ramgur has at some remote period seen better days: at present it has little of magnificence to boast of; but although its inhabitants have been stripped of all their worldly greatness, they seem to have held fast to the faith of their forefathers; they still retain a temple and a tank for prayer and pious washing: indeed its recluse situation, with its large and wide spreading trees, give it an air well suited to the solemnity of Hindoo worship.'

76, 77 'The Temple of Mandeswara near Chaynpore, Bahar', and 'Interior of the Temple of Mandeswara near Chaynpore, Bahar' (V, *Antiquities of India*, 13 and 22)
22 January 1790. 'Rode out two or three Koass this morng to the hill called Setacurrusooee on which the Hindoos say that Seta when Ram her husband was in pursuit of her stoped to dress her Dinner.' (*Journal*)

'This Temple . . . terminates the top of the hill of Seeta, and was dedicated to Mandeswara, one of the appellations of Maha-Deva. By the accumulated mass under which the Temple is now buried, it appears probable it had originally a spire, similar to many other Hindoo Temples in this part of India; and the peculiar forms of the ornamental parts found near the entrance, strengthen this conjecture. The irregular path on the side of the hill leading up to the Temple is in many places marked with the mouldering remains of ancient Hindoo art.' For Thomas Daniell's sketch of the exterior, see p. 102.

75

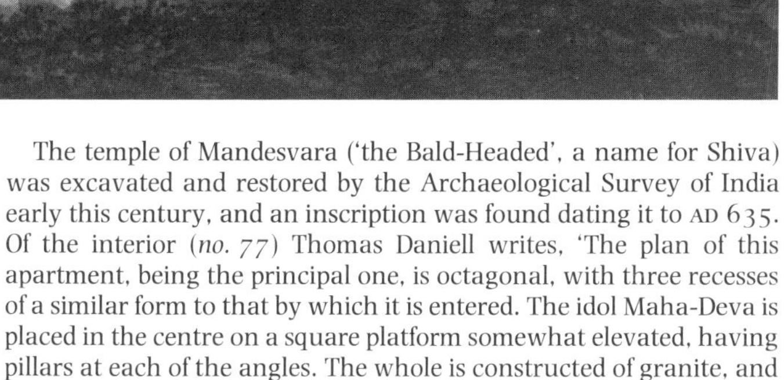

76

The temple of Mandesvara ('the Bald-Headed', a name for Shiva) was excavated and restored by the Archaeological Survey of India early this century, and an inscription was found dating it to AD 635. Of the interior (*no. 77*) Thomas Daniell writes, 'The plan of this apartment, being the principal one, is octagonal, with three recesses of a similar form to that by which it is entered. The idol Maha-Deva is placed in the centre on a square platform somewhat elevated, having pillars at each of the angles. The whole is constructed of granite, and in the ancient Hindoo style.'

This depiction of a Shiva temple with a lingam and yoni would have had great contemporary interest, for a number of British scholars were studying Indian phallic symbols, attempting to link them with the Graeco-Roman Priapus cult and to find a common origin. Charles Townley owned a sculpture of Indian deities seated around a lingam and Richard Payne Knight in 1786 had published a *Discourse on the worship of Priapus and its connection with the Mystic Theology of the Ancients*.

77

78

78 'Exterior of an Eed-gah near Chaynpore, Bahar' (V, *Antiquities of India*, 15)
c.23 January 1790. Chainpur, which was formerly an extensive town, is situated in the western part of Shahabad District and possesses an old fort. The area was inhabited by people from whom the East India Company drew some of its best sepoys. Thomas Twining, posted there as a Company servant in the 1790s, wrote with affection of this 'eminently martial people, easily inflamed, and impatient of control, but with management and firmness, their subordination is easily secured. A more intimate acquaintance with the inhabitant of Cheynpore discovers in his character many excellent qualities which his pride and haughty demeanour conceal from transient observation . . . I reckoned that in case my district were attacked, I could assemble in this part 20,000 men upon whose valour and fidelity I could depend.'

Thomas and William Daniell were more interested in the architecture. 'An Eed-Gah is a place designed for the performance of solemn festivals by the professors of the Mahomedan religion. The interior of this building is extremely plain, and . . . of an open quadrangular form, somewhat resembling the courts before the Musjeds, or Mosques of the Mahomedans . . . This view represents a part of the exterior of the building. The general forms are uncommon, as well as the embellishments, which nevertheless are extremely rich and not inelegant.'

79 'Dhuah Koonde' (IV, *Twenty-Four Landscapes*, 11). *See also colour plate XV*
February 1790. On their way down to the Son River the Daniells stopped to draw Dhuan Kund, the Pool of Smoke, where the Kao River drops down to the plain in a cascade. Waterfalls constantly attracted the artists and Thomas could therefore sympathize with the Hindu veneration for 'those magnificent circumstances in nature', even though he considered it 'superstitious folly'. Water generally, he observed, 'but in hot climates more particularly, is an obvious source of endless comforts and advantages', and would naturally attract 'fabricators of mythological systems'. When it had 'acquired divine attributes, and the sacred fluid was believed capable of washing away the blemishes of sin, we cannot wonder that the unreasoning multitude . . . should behold the foaming torrent, falling in thunder down the precipice, with equal dread and veneration; and imagine

79

the holy haze that fills the surrounding atmosphere must give an extraordinary degree of sanctity to such situations, and consequently a superior efficacy to their ablutional rites. They approach the sacred stream as into the presence of a superior being; and while their corporeal members are really cleansed, they piously believe, that by so close a contact with the divinity their spiritual part must necessarily acquire a corresponding purity.'

Thomas Daniell describes how the visitors to the waterfall pitch their tents close to the water and 'thus form a little society, which becomes a kind of fair, that enables these good people to mingle somewhat of cheerfulness with their devotion'.

80 'Raje Gaut, the Principal Road up to Rotas Ghur, Bahar' (I, *Oriental Scenery*, 5). *See also colour plate XVI*

February 1790. 'Rotas Ghur is the most considerable hill fort in this part of India; it is naturally of great strength, and the weaker parts have been assisted by very strong works.' (See also *nos. 81–83*.)

Rohtasgarh was captured from its Hindu ruler by Sher Khan Sur in 1539. It was eventually surrendered to the British in 1764.

80

81

81 'N.W. View of Rotas Ghur, Bahar' (I, *Oriental Scenery*, 20)
82 'An Antient Hindoo Temple, in the Fort of Rotas, Bahar' (I, *Oriental Scenery*, 11)
83 'Ruins in Rotas Gur, Bahar' (III, *Oriental Scenery*, 2)

February 1790. Within the fort of Rohtasgarh were the remains of a Mughal palace, mosques, and Hindu temples. 'We found the place altogether so agreeable, that we ordered our camp-equipage to be brought to the fort, within which we pitched our tents, and took possession of an old palace then in a state of great dilapidation, yet sufficiently entire to afford us a satisfactory abode for several days. In consequence of its great elevation, we escaped the general annoyance from reptiles to which all persons who inhabit old buildings in India are especially liable; in short, there was nothing to disturb the serenity of our repose save the chattering of legions of monkeys which had colonised the neighbouring glen, inhabiting the trees that grew from the sloping sides of the precipice beneath the fort.' (*The Oriental Annual*, 1835)

'This view of Rotas Ghur [*no. 81*] was taken nearly at the top of the mountain within the works. A temple of the Hindoos, with a considerable flight of steps, formerly crowned the eminence on the

82

left; the upper part of which has been thrown down by the Mahommedans, who erected a mosque near to it, and which in its turn is also become a ruin. No inhabitants are now to be found within the extensive walls of this magnificent fortress.'

During their journey up-country the Daniells had been largely concerned with recording Muslim architecture. Now in Bihar they were continually seeing small Hindu temples, like this one (*no. 82*), whose neat compact shape greatly attracted Thomas Daniell. 'This building, composed of grey granite, is of singular construction, and has the appearance of great antiquity. The Hindoos, who formerly preferred elevated places for their temples, could not, it would seem, resist the temptation of building in this place, the situation being delightful, and water and wood, with every other convenience, abundant.' In 1800 Thomas based a monument to Warren Hastings at Melchet Park on the porch of this little temple (ill. p. 230), and Repton modelled a gateway at the Brighton Pavilion on it.

The palace in the fort (*no. 83*) is one of the few examples of Mughal civil architecture in Bihar. Man Singh, Akbar's Hindu general and Viceroy of Bengal and Bihar, who strengthened the fortifications, is said to have built it in about 1607.

83

84

84, 85 'An Hindoo Temple, at Deo, in Bahar', and 'Part of the Interior of an Hindoo Temple, at Deo, in Bahar' (V, *Antiquities of India*, 5 and 6)

c.February 1790. 'Deo is a small village in the neighbourhood of Gya, in the province of Bahar. The Temple is dedicated to Seeva, and reported to be of considerable antiquity, although from the nature of the material of which it is built (being of hard grey granite) it is but little impaired by time: a coping, however, projecting from above the pilasters, had evidently, at some former period, sheltered the entrance; the ornamental parts in some places have likewise given way. It appears to have had formerly a covering of stucco, the remaining part of which is become of a much darker colour than the stone.' The temple was probably built in the fifteenth century.

'The inside of this building, like the outside, is altogether formed of grey granite; but does not appear to have been incrusted with stucco. In the centre of the ceiling is a sculptured Lotos, supporting an iron chain to which several bells are attached: it being customary for the Hindoos to give notice of their approach to the sacred apartment by ringing of bells.'

86 'Interior of a Temple, near Muddunpore' (V, *Antiquities of India*, 16)

March 1790. Between Deo and Gaya the artists stopped at Madanpur, a small town with a desecrated temple. They note: 'its situation is so recluse that it might have been expected the Hindoos here would have escaped the insolence of Mahomedan usurpation; unfortunately for them it happened otherwise, for after suffering in common with their countrymen from these intolerant invaders, they had the mortification to find their principal Temple, which is the subject of this view, polluted, and their sacred idols defaced.'

For the Daniells this was fortunate, as they could enter the temple to examine its architecture without fear of offending worshippers.

85

86

87

87 'View of Gyah, an Hindoo Town, in Bahar' (III, *Oriental Scenery*, 15). *See also colour plate XVII*

88 'The Sacred Tree of the Hindoos at Gyah, Bahar' (I, *Oriental Scenery*, 15)

March 1790. 'Gyah is a place of great antiquity, much resorted to by religious Hindoos; there being many temples of high celebrity in the town, and on the neighbouring eminences: the whole together forming a very interesting effect . . .'

In addition to the Vishnupad Temple, which had only recently been built, many ancient shrines existed which were visited by the pilgrims as they made a tour of the whole sacred area. South of the city is Bodhgaya, site of the Buddha's enlightenment.

This aquatint with its subtle tones of blue and green is one of the most lyrical of Thomas Daniell's prints.

The Akshai Vata, or undying banyan tree, to which pilgrims make the last offering of their tour, lies half a mile (about 800 m) to the south-west of the Vishnupad Temple. Thomas had noticed temples under banyans in villages, 'where frequently may be observed fragments of mutilated idols, the work of Mahommedan intolerance, which are again often collected by the patient Hindoos, and, though defaced, are still regarded with veneration.

This Tree, the Bramins assure the people, proceeds from another more sacred one, which is growing within a very ancient temple, under ground, in the fort of Allahabad; and, notwithstanding the distance is not less than two hundred miles [320 km], the story obtains an easy belief from credulous devotees, who cheerfully pay the sacred fee that admits them to a ceremonial adoration of it.'

88

89, 90 'S.W. View of the Fakeer's Rock in the River Ganges, near Sultaungunge', and 'S.E. View of the Fakeer's Rock in the River Ganges, near Sultaungunge' (V, *Antiquities of India*, 9 and 10). *See also colour plate XVIII*

1790. 'The Fakeer's rock ... consists of several masses of grey granite, and was formerly a point of land projecting from the shore, but by the violence of the current is now become perfectly insular.' 'This assemblage of rocks has been long considered as one of the most sacred places on the River Ganges, and much resorted to by the religious Hindoos, not only for its reported sanctity, but on account of a much celebrated figure of Narayan [Brahma], over which is erected a building, probably, either to honour or preserve the idol. There are several other figures of Narayan to be seen here, as well as those of Seeva, Vichnou, and Sooroj.'

Fanny Parks anchored nearby in November 1836. 'The abode of the Fakir is on a high bold rock, rising abruptly in the midst of the stream, completely isolated; the temple is placed on the very summit; there are four small temples also a little below; some large trees spring from the crevices of the rock; the whole reflected in the Ganges, with the village of Janghira beyond . . . We passed over in a little boat to see this temple; the fakirs showed it with great good will, and gained a small reward. There is a remarkably fine tree, the plumeria alba, springing from the side of the rock, the goolachin or junglee champa, as the natives call it.'

89

90

91

92

93

91 'Ruins at the Antient City of Gour formerly on the Banks of the River Ganges' (I, *Oriental Scenery*, 4)
92 'A Minar at Gour' (V, *Antiquities of India*, 23)
c.September 1791. Gaur was the capital of Bengal under its ancient Hindu kings and after 1200 under Muslim rulers, but an outbreak of plague in 1575 caused it to be abandoned. Thomas Daniell notes that the city 'is nearly overgrown with jungle (i.e. reeds, thorns, and close underwood). The Ganges, which formerly washed its walls, now runs eight or ten miles [some 15 km] to the westward of it.'

Samuel Davis almost certainly accompanied the Daniells to Gaur: he recorded the Kotwali Gate and in his drawing (p. 104) it may well be Thomas who is seated sketching. Thomas's aquatint probably shows the Dakhil Gate on the north of the citadel. He includes a wild pig in the tall grass in the foreground: the *Oriental Annual* of 1835 includes a vivid (but perhaps imaginary) account of the shooting of such an animal at Gaur by William Daniell.

The builder of the minar (*no. 92*), a five-storeyed tower of brick and granite, is unknown. It may have been erected by Firuz Shah (ruled 1490) or by Husain Shah (ruled 1493–1519) to commemorate his victories in Assam. Thomas Daniell had no idea. Fanny Parks thought that this 'column of solid masonry, within which winds a circular stair' might have been a hunting tower, like the one at Fatehpur Sikri, 'from the top of which the emperor massacred his game at leisure'.

She was delighted with the setting of the ruins at Gaur, 'covered with the silk cotton tree, the date palm, and various other trees; and there was a large sheet of water, covered by high jungle grass, rising far above the heads of the men who were on foot. On the clear dark purple water of a large tank floated the lotus in the wildest luxuriance; over all the trees the jungle climbers twisted and twined; and the parasitical plants, with their red flowers, were in bunches on the branches.'

93 'View taken on the Esplanade, Calcutta' (II, *Oriental Scenery*, 1)
c.January-February 1792. 'The Esplanade lies between Fort William to the south, and the town of Calcutta to the north, which are distant about half a mile [800 m]; Cheringhee on the east, and on the west the river Hooghley, a branch of the Ganges. The Orphan House, with towers at the angles, is seen on the opposite side of the river, which is here three quarters of a mile [1,200 m] wide. Ships of considerable burthen come up as high as Calcutta. The Dutch East Indiamen, French and Danes, proceed many miles further to their respective settlements of Chinsura, Chandernagore, and Serampore.'

The Esplanade or Maidan was a popular place for the evening stroll. The wide stretch of river was lively with shipping of many different kinds, from pleasure-boats to great East Indiamen.

Thomas Daniell states that 'This and the following views of Calcutta were taken in the year 1792', but his memory would seem to have failed him: as we shall see (*nos. 96, 98*), some of the drawings had clearly been made earlier, before he and William left on their tour up the country.

94

95

94 'The Council House, Calcutta' (II, *Oriental Scenery*, 3)
January-February 1792. 'The Council House [of 1764] stands on the north side of the Esplanade, and is the principal place at the Presidency of Bengal, where the affairs of the English East India Company are transacted. The house, with pillars [the Accountant General's Office], has an example of a Virandah, or open Corridor; a mode of building of considerable utility in tropical climates. The roofs of the houses in Calcutta are generally terraced, and on which it is not unusual to walk after sunset; they are also of great advantage in collecting rain in those places where the water is not good.'

This part of the city was also illustrated in the early *Views of Calcutta* (*no. 13*). Thomas Twining in 1792 was greatly impressed by it. 'A range of magnificent buildings, including the Governor's palace, the council-house, the supreme court-house, the Accountant General's office, etc. extended eastward from the river, and then turning at a right angle to the south, formed, on two sides, the limit both of the city and plain. Nearly all these buildings were occupied by the civil and military officers of Government, either as their public offices or private residences. They were all white, their roofs invariably flat, surrounded by light colonnades, and their fronts relieved by lofty columns supporting deep verandahs. They were all separated from each other, each having its own small enclosure, in which, at a little distance from the house, were the kitchen, cellars, storerooms etc. and a large folding gate and porter's lodge at the entrance.'

95 'The Writers' Buildings, Calcutta' (II, *Oriental Scenery*, 4)
January–February 1792. 'The Writers' Buildings, so called from being the residence of the junior part of the Gentlemen in the service of the English East India Company. Immediately beyond this Edifice is the old Court House; the road leads on to the Loll Bazar; the obelisk was erected by Governor Holwell, in commemoration of the dreadful circumstance which happened in the prison called the Blackhole in the year 1756.'

Thomas Twining in 1792 describes Holwell's Monument: 'At the angle by which I entered the tank square, as the great area was called, stood an obelisk in a neglected ruinous state. As it was only a few yards out of my way, I went up to it. From my very early years few things had filled my mind with more horror than the very name of the Black Hole of Calcutta, although the exact history of this tragic celebrity was unknown to me. With peculiar force was this impression revived, when, on deciphering an almost obliterated inscription, I found that the column which I beheld was the monument which had been erected to the memory of the victims of that horrible massacre. A native who accompanied me pointed to the part of the fort south of the principal gate in which the fatal dungeon itself was situated.'

This scene can be linked up with two prints in the early *Views of Calcutta*, *nos.* 4 and 5.

96 'Part of Cheringhee, Calcutta' (II, *Oriental Scenery*, 6)
'1792' (1787). 'Cheringhee is situated on the east side of the Esplanade [*no.* 93], and, though formerly separated, may now be considered as making a part of the town of Calcutta. The houses, which are of brick, stuccoed, and afterwards coloured, are inhabited by opulent English gentlemen, and are well constructed to counteract, as much as possible, the inconveniences of so hot a climate.'

This is another print after the drawing used for *no. 10* in the *Views of Calcutta*, which Thomas Daniell had made in 1787.

OVERLEAF:

97 'Govinda Ram Mittee's Pagoda, Calcutta' (II, *Oriental Scenery*, 5)
January–February 1792. 'The Pagoda, or Hindoo Temple, which is dedicated to Seeva, was built by Govinda Ram Mittee, a native merchant, residing in the neighbourhood of Calcutta, but never completely finished. It is a modern work, principally of brick, and in a mixed style of architecture. The Tank is a necessary appendage to buildings of this nature, ablution being a ceremony that very frequently occurs in the religious duties of an Hindoo.' (See also *no. 7*.)

This scene in the Chitpore Bazaar is typical of the outskirts of Calcutta even today, with water buffalo swimming in the tanks and village huts with curved thatched roofs.

98 'View on the Chitpore Road, Calcutta' (II, *Oriental Scenery*, 2)
'1792' (1786–88?). 'In this view on the Chitpore road (taken in the Monsoon season) appears the house of a native Bengal merchant; the style of architecture in its ornamental parts is Mahommedan, except in the turret, which is an unsuccessful attempt at the Grecian, as introduced by the Portugueze. These incongruities very frequently occur in modern Indian buildings, whose owners have intercourse with Europeans.

Part of a Bazar, or market, is seen, and a small Hindoo temple of modern construction.'

For the Chitpore Bazaar, see *no. 7*.

If Thomas's reference to the monsoon season is correct, it seems probable that the present engraving, like *no. 96*, was based on an earlier drawing made between 1786 and 1788. By the time the rains began in 1792, the Daniells were in South India.

96

97

98

The South
March 1792 to February 1793

WITH THEIR FUNDS RE-ESTABLISHED, Thomas Daniell now planned a tour of South India. Compared with Upper India the extreme South was far less known to the British and few travellers' descriptions of it existed. Hodges while staying there had been unable to tour the interior, as Haidar Ali, the ruler of Mysore, had been threatening Madras and dominating the surrounding countryside. The Daniells therefore had no feelings of rivalry and were free to plan their own itinerary. Events were helping them to formulate their plans.

While the Daniells were in Bhagalpur in 1790–91 news of the Third Mysore War had reached them. Haidar Ali's son, Tipu, had become ruler and was once again challenging the East India Company's power. The war under General Medows had dragged on but in January 1791 the Governor-General, Lord Cornwallis, had taken over its direction, and in March Bangalore capitulated to the Grand Army. Instead of continuing towards Tipu's capital at Seringapatam, Cornwallis had prudently spent most of the following year in neutralizing Tipu's hill forts (the 'droogs'), which lay to the south and east of Bangalore and were threatening his supply lines. By February 1792, when the Daniells were getting ready to leave Calcutta, Cornwallis appeared ready to attack Seringapatam. The campaign was arousing intense interest among the British and it was obvious to the Daniells that a first-hand depiction of the places associated with it could have great popular appeal.

On 10 March 1792 the two artists set sail for Madras on board the pilot sloop *Hastings*, taking with them their stock of drawings and unsold oils. At the mouth of the river they transferred to the East Indiaman *Dutton*, which arrived at Madras on 29 March (*no.* 99). Cornwallis, they discovered, had negotiated a peace treaty and two of Tipu's sons had been handed over to the British as hostages. The artists at once made hasty arrangements for their tour and set off in palanquins during the afternoon of 9 April. This time they had a train of forty-eight servants. For travelling they had two palanquins, each with eleven bearers, two horses with two syces or grooms, a bullock cart and three pack bullocks with four drivers to carry the tents and baggage. There were seven bearers to carry the provisions and the chickens, two coolies to carry the drawing tables and another the cot. Their personal servants consisted of a head

Three of the Daniells' servants, including a 'palanquin boy' (top) and 'second *dubash*' or interpreter – the latter sketch (above), less accomplished, probably an early work of William's. (Private collection)

servant, a *dubash* to handle money matters, a cook, two orderlies, two tent pitchers, a Portuguese servant named Francis and a Muslim boy. In view of the length and rigours of their tour it was a modest retinue.

The Daniells followed the route by which the Grand Army had set out just over a year before in February 1791. Passing St Thomas's Mount, they travelled south-west through the flat paddy fields studded with coconut palms. They spent the night in a travellers' rest-house (known in South India as a 'choultry'). On the second day a downpour of rain flooded their tent. Continuing on their way they soon encountered signs of the recent war, for they overtook a procession of covered litters slowly making its way to Bangalore to bring back the sick and wounded. On 11 April at Perambur they saw their first example of a richly carved South Indian temple. Nearby were tanks where in March and April an image of the god is floated on a raft. Continuing westwards they reached Kanchipuram ('Conjeeveram') with its vast temple – 'the most considerable we have seen', wrote William.

Soon afterwards the country began to change, the flat landscape giving way to rocky hills surrounding Arcot, the capital of the Muslim Nawab of the Carnatic, which was famous for its capture by Clive in 1751 during the second Anglo-French War. They rested there for a short time as the baggage-bullocks were tired after struggling through the sandy bed of the Paliar River. Then they continued to Vellore with its great fort surrounded by a moat. By 20 April they had reached the Baramahal Hills, a slanting range of rocky country stretching from north-east to south-west at an angle to the Bangalore plateau. The Daniells crossed it through the pass of Ambur, from which they had 'an uncommonly beautiful view'. The next day they met a great convoy of three to four hundred litters carrying wounded European soldiers back to Vellore hospital: 'the scenes grow busy as we approach the Grand Army'. During the next week a number of minor disasters befell them. A coolie tripped, breaking two bottles of madeira – 'a serious consideration', wrote William; the next day the *dubash* absconded taking the servants' money with him; and four days later they themselves were robbed of clothing during the night. However on 2 May they reached Bangalore via Kolar (*no. 100*), Nursapur and Ouscottah and they were shown 'the places where our batteries were and the part that was breached and stormed'.

During May the artists were moving through the dramatic hilly country south of Bangalore (*nos. 101, 102, XIX, XX*), visiting the various hill forts where Tipu's soldiers had held out against the British. Going south they visited Hosur (*no. 103*), which commanded the northernmost end of the pass used by Cornwallis for his supply route. They took a sepoy with them as some of Tipu's men were still lurking in the area. The forts of Anchetti, Naldurgum, Huriya, Chinna Raidurga, and Rayakottai (*no. 104, XXI*) were visited in turn, as well as Verapadrug (*no. 105*), Krishnagiri and Jagdeo (*no. 106*). The Daniells could not fail to be impressed by the vast rocks which appeared unscalable. The whole area was wonderfully picturesque. 'Rocks of all forms and sizes, tinted as one could wish & grouping with the wild aloe made very rich foregrounds. The clouds now & then broke over the tops of some of the ragged hills which improved them in shape as well as colour.' Most impressive of all was Sankaridrug (*no. 107, XXII*). The Daniells set out at dawn to climb this great rocky mass, ate their breakfast on the way up, made a number of drawings and returned by 1 o'clock. One stands amazed at their physical

energy, for they were climbing these great hills during the heat of May. Although the 'droogs' were also drawn by the army officers Captains Allan and Colebrooke and by the artist Robert Home, it is the engravings of the Daniells which best convey the impressive scale of the hills and the difficulties that Cornwallis's army experienced in capturing them.

The next month was spent in a very different manner. From picturesque scenery, the Daniells now turned their attention to picturesque architecture and the historic monuments well known to the British public through the exploits of Clive and the wars with the French. They visited the great temples at Trichengodu, the temple of Kailasanatha at the foot of the hill and the upper temple of Ardhanaresvara which is reached by a long toil up the rock on which a huge serpent is carved. The Daniells were told by the villagers that they were the first Europeans to reach the upper temple. They moved on to Trichinopoly where military operations against the French had taken place in 1752–54. The besieged city had been relieved by Clive and Stringer Lawrence had accepted the surrender of the French at Srirangam on the opposite side of the river. Although the Daniells knew that views of the fort and the rock would appeal to the British public (*nos. 108–111, XXIII*), they themselves were more interested in the great temple at Srirangam, which extends over 23 acres (about 9 hectares) with twenty-one great temple-gateways or *gopurams*. From Trichinopoly they travelled south to Madura, passing through Dindigul and Atur (no. 112).

The Daniells reached Madura on 3 July and here they were surrounded by a plethora of temples and palaces. The Great Temple (*no. 113*) must have amazed them with its intricate complex of high walls, vast gateways and numerous shrines filled with fantastic images. Little has changed since they visited it and carefully drew the Thousand-Pillared Hall with its rearing horses, elegant gods and voluptuous damsels (*no. 114*). They were also deeply impressed by the palace built by Tirumala Nayyak in about 1636 (nos. 116–118, XXIV), where the sturdy pillars and vaulted roof give the impression of a great Norman cathedral. The fort, however, had fallen into disrepair (*no. 115*). Near Madura they visited the temple of Skandamalai with its great *gopuram* standing silhouetted against the hill of Murukan. In this area they were seeing some of the greatest of the South Indian temples which contrasted so dramatically with the Mughal architecture which they had been exploring in North India.

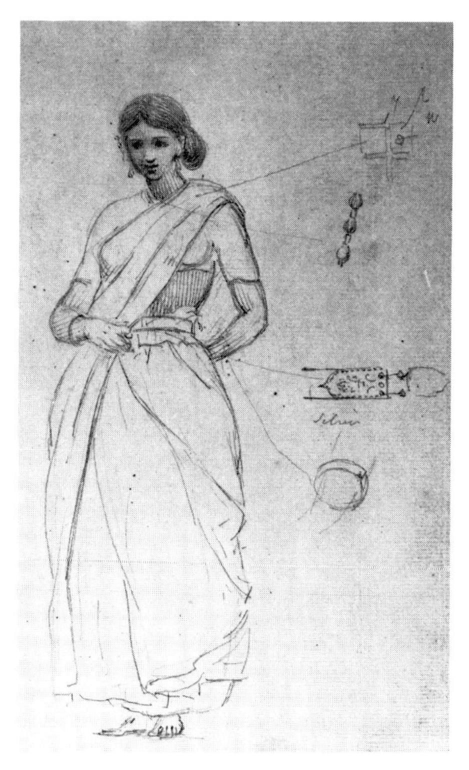

Pencil sketch of a woman, showing the care with which Thomas Daniell noted details of textiles and jewellery for future use in his oils and aquatints. (Private collection)

After Madura, yet another phase of their journey opened up. They were leaving these man-made wonders and entering an area where they were to marvel at the 'sublimity' of the scenery. Like the Garhwal mountains, this region was still unmapped and unadministered by the British: the Tinnevelly District, through which the Daniells travelled south, with a great line of hills on their right, was not surveyed until 1807. After Srivilliputtur (*no. 119, XXV*) and Sivagiri (*no. 120*) the cultivated plain at the foot of the hills began to give way to rougher country with great forests and hills. At Kattalam there was a series of magnificent waterfalls (*no. 121*). The artists spent the latter part of July and August exploring the forests around Ambasamudram and visiting further waterfalls on the Chittar and Tambrapani Rivers. The remote falls of Vannar Thurthum and Papanasam fascinated them, especially the latter with its steep approach up fallen rocks and its carvings before which pilgrims prostrated themselves (*no. 122, XXVI*). They continued south, and as they approached Cape Comorin the scenery grew grander than ever with the great peak of

Detail of Robert Home's painting of the surrender of Tipu Sultan's sons in February 1792. The artist stands at the far left, with a portfolio under his arm; one of the hostage princes is on the right. Behind are some of Tipu's rocketmen, with rockets on the end of long poles. Home worked up this oil in Madras in 1793–94 from sketches made at the time, some of which Thomas Daniell saw and copied. (National Army Museum)

Mahendra Giri at Kalakad wreathed in clouds (*no. 123, XXVII*). Throughout this part of their journey they experienced all the romantic thrills of the sublime and the picturesque which were so valued at this period.

From the southern tip of India the two artists now made their way back to Madras along the eastern coast, halting at a number of famous temples on the way. They visited Ramesvaram, where the temple stands on a spur of land projecting towards Ceylon, and they camped in the choultry washed by the sea. At Tanjore they were greatly impressed by the Brihadisvara Temple, where a huge stone carving of the bull Nandi stands in the courtyard (*nos. 124, 125, XXVIII*), and they also saw the Raja's palace. Continuing north they passed Gingee with its fort and strange towered palace. Mahabalipuram's temples and richly carved rocks provided them with many subjects (*nos. 127, 128, XXIX*). Eventually they arrived back in Madras in November 1792.

Once again they settled down to the hard work of completing oils ready for another lottery and making drawings of the city itself. Like Calcutta, Madras had been developing fast during the late eighteenth century, although the threat from Mysore had hindered expansion outside the Fort area. The Nawab of Arcot had built a fine palace for himself at Chepauk facing the sea to the south. The Fort had been enlarged and the Fort House, the Governor's residence, had been repaired. Inside the Fort were streets of elegant houses. Rooms at the Pantheon and the Exchange were used for assemblies and a Coffee Tavern had been opened. Knowing that Madras residents would be interested in views of their city, just as the Calcutta inhabitants had been in theirs, the two Daniells made drawings of the Fort, Government House, the Armenian Bridge, Black Town and the Assembly Rooms on the Race Ground (*nos. 129–133*). A lottery was advertised in the *Madras Courier* on 20 and 27 December 1792 and the draw fixed for 18 February 1793.

At the end of January, Thomas despatched to England the drawings which he and his nephew had made during their southern tour. They also paid another short visit to Mahabalipuram, probably with the artist Robert Home. This young man had accompanied the army of Lord Cornwallis as war-artist throughout the Third Mysore War; he had been present at the surrender of the hostage princes, and had made first-hand drawings of Tipu's soldiers and rocketmen. Thomas Daniell not unnaturally was interested in seeing these since he himself had not had close contact with Tipu's troops, and he made a number of copies from Home's sketches recording costume and uniforms.

The lottery was once again a success. The paintings of the South were supplemented by paintings left over from the Calcutta sale, making a total of sixty-eight oils and eight drawings. Richard Chase, the Mayor of Madras, is known to have acquired at least ten of Thomas Daniell's oils.

For the map, see p. 189.

XIX (101)

XX (102)

XXI (104)

XXII (107)

XXIII (109)

xxiv (116)

XXV (119)

XXVI (122)

XXVII (123)

xxviii (125)

XXIX (127)

99 'The Government House, Fort St George' (II, *Oriental Scenery*, 9) *March 1792*. The Daniells reached Madras on 29 March 1792 and hastily began to organize their tour of South India. They had little time to make any drawings and this aquatint, like their other views of the city, was based on a watercolour made early in 1793 (see *no. 129*) after their return there.

Madras was the first of the important British settlements of the East India Company. It was founded in 1639 and a small fort was built in 1644. That was later enlarged, and within it Government House stood in its own fortified enclosure. 'The Government House', Thomas Daniell writes, 'is within the Fort; here the business of the English East India Company is transacted, but the residence of the Governor is at the distance of a mile and a quarter [2 km] from Madras. The colonnade to the right leads down to the sea gate, where merchandise of various kinds is seen continually passing to and from the ships in the roads.'

When the Daniells were in Madras the Governor frequently lived outside the Fort in his garden house on the Cooum River to the south of the city. The Sea Gate has now been made into a museum. Amongst its collections are paintings by British artists of the Nawabs of the Carnatic, Chinese export-ware made specially for the East India Company, and the silver-gilt alms plate presented to St Mary's Church by Governor Elihu Yale in 1687.

100

100 'An Antique Reservoir near Colar, in the Mysore' (V, *Antiquities of India*, 14)
c.25 April 1792. 'This stone cistern, which is very singular in its form, and in its style of decoration, was evidently intended for the purpose of containing water. It is situated near the high road not far from Colar; it was probably at some former period attached to a Choultry [travellers' rest-house], and place of residence of the Brahmins, though now nearly left without accompaniments. What remains is in the style of the antient architecture of the Hindoos. The great advantage of such an accommodation to travellers on the parched plains of this part of India, must be obvious, and it displays both the taste and benevolence of its author.'

Kolar today is chiefly known for its gold mines.

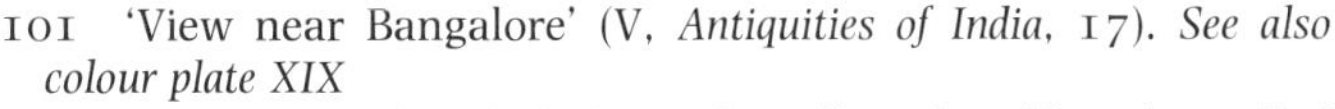

101 'View near Bangalore' (V, *Antiquities of India*, 17). *See also colour plate XIX*

1 May 1792. 'Spent the whole day at the Hills to the Sd [southward] of Bangalore where we collected several Scenes.' (*Journal*)

'The neighbourhood of Bangalore is remarkable for the frequent appearance of the remains of antient Hindoo architecture. Nearly in the centre of this view is a temple, but at present without an idol. On the left is the Chackra or Discus of Vishnoo placed horizontally, supported by a pillar, both executed in stone; and on the right is a pavilion very neatly executed, which probably was the place for exhibiting to the multitude the idol belonging to the adjoining temple. Further on to the right is a stone pillar, on the top of which on particular occasions was placed the sacred fire.'

102

102 'Entrance to a Hindoo Temple, near Bangalore' (V, *Antiquities of India*, 18). *See also colour plate XX*

1 May 1792. 'The entrance to this Temple has a very striking effect from the size and singularity of the mythological sculpture wrought in stone, which appears in the court before the Temple. On the right is the trident of Maha-deva [Shiva], and not far from it are two examples of the Chackra of Vishnoo, supported perpendicularly. Here are also pillars and altars for various religious purposes. . . . The passage leading to the interior, which is partly excavated, is so completely choked up with large stones as to be inaccessible. This place having now no establishment for religious duty, is accordingly deserted.'

South Indian temples frequently stand in the midst of a large enclosure which contains various buildings such as pilgrims' rest-houses and covered halls for sheltering images, as well as pillars for lamps and bells, and the sacred symbols of the gods. In the background here are the pavilion, pillar and chakra seen in *no. 101*.

The 'singularity' of objects was an important aspect of the picturesque. There is little doubt that the trisula or trident of Shiva and the chakra of Vishnu intrigued Thomas Daniell for this reason. When in 1799 the connoisseur Thomas Hope asked him for a painting which would embrace various aspects of Indian architecture, these strange forms at once came into the artist's mind (see p. 227).

101

103 'Ousoor, in the Mysore' (III, *Oriental Scenery*, 14)
4 May 1792. 'Had a very pleasant ride to Oosoor, the Country the whole way exceedingly beautiful. As a number of Tipoo's People were in the vicinity in the Fort, Cap. C. gave us a Seapoy to accompany us to the Hill abt a Mile S. E. of the Fort – on the Top are several hindoo Temples.' (*Journal*)

'The fort of Ousoor in the Mysore country, is built on tolerably even ground, though considerably elevated. The town is surrounded by an almost impenetrable hedge; the outer works of the fort are constructed much in the European manner, and were undergoing such repairs and additions as would have made it a very strong place, when it was taken without much resistance by Major Gowdie in July, one thousand seven hundred and ninety-two [actually 1791], during the third campaign of earl Cornwallis. This view was drawn from an eminence south of the fort.'

The Daniells' aquatint catches excellently the dry rocky country of the Bangalore plateau. The capture of the fort of Hosur was of great importance to Cornwallis during his campaign against Tipu Sultan as it guarded the northern end of the pass through the Baramahal Hills, on the supply route used by the British from the the Carnatic to Bangalore.

104 'Ryacotta, in the Barramah'l' (III, *Oriental Scenery*, 12). *See also colour plate XXI*
9 May 1792. 'Ryacotta is one of the highest and strongest hill forts of the Barramah'l'. Like Hosur it was captured in July 1791 by Major Gowdie, 'who soon carried by assault the lower works which enclosed the Pettah' (the commercial suburb outside a fortress); the Killedar, or commandant, 'after a slight resistance, gave up this lofty spacious fort, which ought to have yielded only to famine and a tedious blockade'.

Rayakottai commanded the southern end of the pass whose northern end was guarded by Hosur. Thomas Daniell proudly shows the British flag flying in the fortifications to the left.

The countryside looks little different today. Although the main buildings have fallen into disrepair, the line of the intricate fortifications can still be traced along the contours of the great hills.

104

105

105 'Verapadroog, in the Barramah'l' (III, *Oriental Scenery*, 13)
11 May 1792. 'My Uncle being indisposed I went up to the Pettah [see *no. 104*] of Verapadroog which is nearly on the top of the hill to pay a visit to Lieut Grace commandg there. The rode up very romantic – passed thro' five Gates before I reached the Pettah, all small with much curious scenery about them – a Kiludar of Tippoo's in the Fort selling & carrying away the Grain that had been given up.' (*Journal*)

'Verapadroog, with respect to its form and situation, is one of the most romantic forts of the Barramah'l. Its sides are very thickly clothed with wood a considerable way up, and the lower part is so surrounded by an impenetrable jungle, that the tygers which are said to be very numerous here, find a secure and undisturbed shelter.'

This is one of the few occasions when Thomas is referred to as being 'indisposed'. Both men were remarkably strong and healthy, and William makes no complaints about climbing the great rocky 'droogs' during the summer heat.

The South Indian word 'droog' for a great fortified hill early became absorbed into the English language. As Captain Bellew, looking back in 1843, wrote, 'Long before the period of my departure arrived – indeed I may say almost from infancy – I had been inoculated by my mother, my great uncles, and sundry parchment-faced gentlemen who frequented our house, with a sort of Indomania . . . What respect did the sonorous names of Bangalore and Cuddalore, and Nundy Droog and Severn Droog and Hookahburdars and Soontaburdars, and a host of others, excite in our young minds.'

106 'Jag Deo & Warrangur, Hill Forts in the Barramah'l' (III, *Oriental Scenery*, 11)
15 May 1792. 'Had a pleasant Journey to Jag Deo, a hill Fort abt 7 miles [*c.* 11 km] to the Eastd of Kishnagherry – pitched our Tent under the shade of Tamarind trees a little to Westd of the Fort the Walls of which are extensive – but few inhabitants in the Village – the Fort in a ruinous state.' (*Journal*)

'Jag Deo, and Warrangur, are two of the twelve Hill Forts, or Barramah'l, which were in the possession of the late Sultaun Tippoo; these are of the lesser class, but, like most of the hill forts, are strongly fortified quite to their rocky summits. The approach to them being extremely difficult, they were considered as very strong situations; but were, nevertheless, given up to the English. . . . without resistance.'

107 'Sankry Droog' (IV, *Twenty-Four Landscapes*, 7). *See also colour plate XXII*
24 May 1792. 'The morning Cloudy – our Journey to Sankry Durgum

106

pleasant (abt 15 Miles [24 km]). Waited on Lieut MacDonald who introduced us to Major Cuppage commanding at Sankry Droog with whom we dined. Pitched near the East Gate of the Pettah [see *no. 104*].
25 May. At day break we began to ascend the Droog – the road the whole way up, pretty good – rough steps tho' in part so slippery from their not being horizontally laid, that obliged us to move with Caution – took our breakfast with us. Descended the Rock abt 10 C. found our thighs a little tired before we reached the bottom – the Day cloudy which to us was a fortunate circumstance. On the Top are several reservoirs of good Water which we were informed was sufficient to supply 5,000 men for Six Months – there are also Granaries for Rice, Sugar, Ghee, Oil, Powder &c. In the Oil Granary our men caught two Young Monkies that must have been in some time as they appeared almost starved.' (*Journal*)

'This view is taken from the north west side of Sankry Droog, one of the largest of those fortified hills that occur so frequently in the Carnatic ... The fortress in which the spectator is placed seems elevated almost into the clouds; its sides are in many parts formed of perpendicular cliffs; it is moreover surrounded with every impediment, natural or artificial, that can render access either impossible or difficult; and all this is to enable one little tyrant to resist the hostility of another, or to favour his own projects of vengeance or plunder.'

107

108, 109 'The Rock of Tritchinopoly, taken on the River Cauvery', and 'The Great Pagoda, Tritchinopoly' (II, *Oriental Scenery*, 19 and 20). *See also colour plate XXIII*

5 June 1792. 'Had a pleasant ride this morning to Tritchinopoly were we were welcomed by Lt Campbell of the Artillery. . . . Mr C— went with us to the Top of the Rock, from whence we had a good general Idea of the surrounding Country – an easy ascent all the way up.' (*Journal*)

Thomas Daniell devoted four aquatints to Trichinopoly, since the rock and fort had become a popular symbol of British military prowess in India. Muhammad Ali, whose claim as Nawab of the Carnatic the British favoured, was besieged there by the French, who supported his rival, Chanda Sahib. The young Captain Robert Clive carried out a daring diversion by capturing Chanda Sahib's capital of Arcot, and then in 1752 raised the siege of Trichinopoly in collaboration with Major Stringer Lawrence. It was not until 1763, with the Treaty of Paris, that Muhammad Ali was recognized as Nawab.

'This view [*no. 108*] is taken on the north side from the river Cauvery in the dry season. The building to the right on the western extremity of the rock is an ancient Hindoo temple, held in great veneration by the votaries of the religion; and the lesser one on the summit, a Choultry, commanding a very rich and extensive prospect. Many small Choultries and places of worship also embellish the banks of the river.'

The temple had been built by a Madura Nayyak ruler in 1660–70. *No. 109* is a dramatic end-on view of the building, which is seen in profile half-way down the rock in *nos. 108 and 111*. 'This Pagoda, or temple, is a south western view of the same edifice, which, taken from the north, appears in the preceding plate. Its exterior form is very much unlike the style that generally prevails in the Hindoo temples: being remarkably plain, and without any decoration excepting the top of the walls, along which are arranged idols of various denominations; and that part of its interior which may be entered by Europeans retains the same unornamented appearance.

This view is taken from an elevated situation on a part of the rock where many of the Bramins reside.'

111

110 'View in the fort of Tritchinopoly' (II, *Oriental Scenery*, 21)

110

111 'South East View of Tritchinopoly' (II, *Oriental Scenery*, 23) *c.5 June 1792*. 'The fort of Tritchinopoly belongs to the nabob of the Carnatic, but is garrisoned by the English. Its walls are nearly four miles [6.5 km] in extent, and surrounded by a broad and deep ditch. There are several tanks here of excellent water; the one seen in this view [*no. 110*] is principally used by the Hindoos for ablution, where persons of all ages and of different sexes assemble together to perform that religious ceremony.'

At the top of the rock is a small mandapam or pavilion up to which the Daniells climbed (see *no. 108*) and obtained a magnificent view of the surrounding countryside. On the west side of the rock is a large sacred tank with a mandapam in the centre where the temple deity is housed during certain festivals.

In *no. 111*, Thomas Daniell writes, the temple 'is represented on that part by which it is entered. The numerous flights of steps, and different buildings to be passed through, both open and enclosed, in ascending the rock, give an awful and grand effect to its approach. The buildings higher up are the Choultries attached to the temple, where devout persons resort after performing their religious duties.'

Flights of steps through a passageway lead up to the Shiva temple, the massive complex on the left (see *no. 109*). Cave temples are hollowed out on the sides of the steps and more stairs then lead out on to the exposed face of the rock.

112 'Near Atoor, in the Dindigul District' (IV, *Twenty-Four Landscapes*, 6)
24 June 1792. 'Left Dindigul abt 7 o C & had a most delightful ride to Atoor . . . The Head Man of Atoor, which is a large Village most pleasantly situated, paid his respects to us & brought a present of Fowls, Limes, Eggs, Milk, &c.' (*Journal*)

'This part of the country, though not entirely uncultivated, has a wild and most romantic character; broken into hill and valley, and covered in many parts with thick woods of great extent, giving shelter to herds of elephants, and numerous other wild animals, that would oft-times quit their gloomy retreats, and carry havock and destruction among the plantations of the peasantry, were they not strictly watched by a class of human creatures, whose shaggy forms and ferocious aspect appear sufficient to strike terror into the hearts even of lions and tigers.'

The 'umbrella tree' was prolific in this area. Its canopy is so thorny as to form 'a covering quite impervious to the rays of the sun. In getting under any of these trees, we invariably found the whole surface of the ground . . . covered with thorns, so that, before we could seat ourselves, it was always necessary to sweep the space well, and even as we sat we were frequently exposed to a prickly shower upon the slightest agitation of the tree from the wind.' (*The Oriental Annual*, 1834)

113 115 >

114

113 'An Hindoo Temple, at Madura' (II, *Oriental Scenery*, 16)
July 1792. 'Madura is a place of great antiquity, justly celebrated for its Hindoo temples and choultries. The lofty part of this building is a gate that leads to the principal temple dedicated to the idol Chokee Lingham.'

This aquatint depicts one of the gateways to the Great Temple of Madura which was built by the Nayyak dynasty in the seventeenth century. The Daniells must have marvelled at the intricate temple complex with its vast gateways, courtyards, pillared halls (*no. 114*) and shrines full of fantastic images. The small choultry seen here on the right has disappeared, but the temple is still like a self-contained city seething with people engaged in varied activities. Marriage parties gather round the family priest, small boys have their heads shaved or their ears pierced, worshippers make their offerings and shopkeepers sell jewellery, toys and mementos to the milling crowds.

114 'Tremal Naig's Choultry, Madura' (II, *Oriental Scenery*, 18)
July 1792. 'The Choultry of rajah Tremal Naig [Tirumala Nayyak] is considered as one of the first works of its kind in the south of Hindoostan. . . . [It] consists of one large hall, the ceiling of which is supported by six ranges of columns, about twenty-five feet [*c.* 7.5 m] in height, many of them formed of single stones, and the whole composed of grey granite. This view contains half the centre ile. On the second pillar to the right hand is the effigy of the rajah with three of his wives, to whom, for his munificence, the Hindoos still continue to pay divine honours. Beyond the rajah, and on the pillars opposite to him are other statues representing his family.

The Choultry is an edifice which in the Decan is always found attached to Hindoo temples, and appropriated to the use of the religious; they are likewise erected on the public roads for the accommodation of travellers.'

Today in the Thousand-Pillared Hall the central aisle depicted here is cordoned off by the Archaeological Department, but the side aisles are full of tailors with their treadle sewing machines busily making shorts and blouses for little shops which line the walls.

115 'View in the Fort, Madura' (II, *Oriental Scenery*, 14)
July 1792. 'The principal object in this view is a pavilion situated on the east side of the fort at Madura. It is constructed of stone, and is ascended by a considerable flight of steps. Rajah Tremal Naig is said to have built it for the purpose of viewing the religious processions, and other ceremonies, of the Hindoos. In the distance appears part of the palace [*no. 117*]; many of the buildings in the fort of Madura have suffered considerably by the siege it sustained in the year 1751.'

The fort has now disappeared, together with this sturdy pavilion built in a style similar to that of the palace. This scene seems to have particularly attracted Europeans, as it was singled out as a decorative motif for both Staffordshire-ware and French wallpapers (ills. pp. 228–29).

116

116 'Ruins of the Palace, Madura' (II, *Oriental Scenery*, 17). *See also colour plate XXIV*

117

118

117 'Part of the Palace, Madura' (II, *Oriental Scenery*, 13)

118 'Interior View of the Palace, Madura' (II, *Oriental Scenery*, 15)
3 July 1792. 'Breakfasted at Tappacallum & went to the Old Palace where we spent the Day. Pitched our Tent to the Sd [southward] of the Palace near the Rampart inside the Fort, where we propose remaining during our Stay at Madura.' (*Journal*)

'The Palace of Madura is said to be principally the work of Tremal Naig, rajah of Madura; at least it may be supposed to have been repaired and beautified by him, who was an Hindoo prince of considerable power and wealth, as appears by the many edifices attributed to him in this neighbourhood. In this building appears a great mixture of the Hindoo and Mahommedan styles of architecture, a circumstance not so frequently occurring in this part of India, as on the banks of the Ganges.'

Thomas Daniell appears to have been greatly attracted by the strong, heavy architecture of the palace, the Swarga Vilasa or Celestial Pavilion, which had been built by Tirumala Nayyak in about 1636. It was already in a state of neglect when the Daniells saw it. As a result of an emphatic Minute written in 1858 by Lord Napier, Governor of Madras, it was eventually well restored in 1871–82.

On the west side of the palace (*no. 116*) a few buildings were 'sufficiently in repair to be converted into use by the garrison, as granaries, store-houses, powder magazines, etc.' The whole area has now been restored, including the missing finials, originally covered in gold, that topped the oblong pavilions.

The north-east side of the palace appears in *no. 117*. The arches on the right have now collapsed and the front is bricked up; trees are growing in the open area and small modern buildings have been erected there. The large building on the left, however, which is seen dominating the fort in *no. 115*, still stands.

The interior (*no. 118*) 'is at present of little more use than affording shelter to cattle; formerly, as some report, it was the rajah's hall of audience, though others conjecture it to have been used as a bath, which opinion is chiefly founded on the circumstance of discovering a smoothly stuccoed floor some feet below the present surface, with a circular hole in the centre, apparently for the admission of water. The materials are of stone, not very smoothly wrought, but from several parts still remaining, the interior surface was certainly covered with chunam, or stucco, and richly painted with various colours.'

The vast granite pillars supporting the scalloped arches contrast strangely with the rich decoration of the contemporary Madura temple (*no. 113*). This hall was later used by the British as government offices and law courts.

119

119 'Chevalpettore' (IV, *Twenty-Four Landscapes*, 5). *See also colour plate XXV*

20 July 1792. 'In this view, taken in the district of Tinnevelly, the Fort of Cheval-Pettore is a conspicuous object. The town of that name . . . [is] about a mile distant on the left. . . . Like most of the Carnatic mountains, the hills here rise abruptly out of the plain beneath; a circumstance which, when they are not in extensive masses, gives them a very singular appearance, resembling rocky islands or islets rising out of the ocean. They are of all dimensions, from what is called the Sugar-loaf rock of Trichinopoly [*no. 110*] to Severn Droog; and of these insulated eminences many examples occur in the preceding works. They are generally selected as fortresses, and are of such difficult access, that their perpendicular sides are only to be assailed with success by British intrepidity.

The ramparts of Cheval-pettore are formed of mud, a material very commonly used in India in the construction of walls for various purposes, though to an European ear it conveys no idea of stability. These earthen walls, nevertheless, baked in the fierce rays of an almost vertical sun, have been often put to a severe test by our artillery, and found equal, if not superior, even to masonry.'

Today the fort of Srivilliputtur has disappeared and the forests have dwindled. The quiet town nearby contains a small temple with ceiling paintings and a friendly temple elephant.

120

120 'Shevagurry' (IV, *Twenty-Four Landscapes*, 4)

July 1792. 'Shevagurry [Sivagiri] is a small village, the residence of a Poligar Rajah, tributary to the British government. It is . . . concealed behind the rocky eminence, whereon is placed the temple and choultries that appear in this view. The inhabitants of this part of the country are chiefly rude mountaineers, but little civilised, and as usual much attached to their native hills, which afford them shelter both from their common enemies and those provoked by their insubordination. Should their chief choose at any time to resist the regular claims of government (a circumstance not infrequent), he immediately flies to his hilly fastnesses, whence he is not easily dislodged; and his submission in such cases can only be enforced with much trouble and expence.'

121

121 'The Water-fall at Courtallum, in the Tinnevelly District' (IV, *Twenty-Four Landscapes*, 3)

July 1792. 'The Waterfall at Courtallum, called Tancanche, . . . is accounted by the Hindoos a place of peculiar sanctity. On certain festivals the number of people that resort to this spot from every part of India, is almost incredible; and to accommodate so great a concourse of religious persons, numerous choultries are provided. Some of the buildings of that description appear in this view . . . the grandeur and religious solemnity of the scene is much heightened by a grove of large spreading trees.'

This fall is the lowest of four. For the composition to fit into a horizontal format, the relationship of the various elements has been distorted: though the size of the waterfull is correctly shown by the tiny figures at its foot, in reality seen from this viewpoint it appears far more impressive, about six times as high as the mandapam on the right. The site at Kattalam is now vulgarized with great advertisement hoardings and the mandapam on the right has been extended.

122 'The Water-fall at Puppanassum in the Tinnevelly District' (IV, *Twenty-Four Landscapes*, 2). *See also colour plate XXVI*

August 1792. 'This magnificent cataract is held by Hindoos in great veneration, and is accordingly visited by innumerable devotees. The only approach to it is by a single path on the right hand side of the valley, whence, though near to the fall, it cannot be seen, owing to the interposition of a large mass of rock that projects into the water. The path is continued up the face of this rock by means of a flight of steps; and at the summit a gate is so placed, that all visitors must of necessity pass through it, but which nevertheless readily opens to all who are provided with a small fee for the brahmins that guard the sacred portal.

Nothing can be more grand and impressive than when, on first throwing open the gate, this extraordinary scene bursts upon the sight . . . accompanied by a noise so tremendous, that, comparatively, all other sounds are but whispers.'

Pilgrims threw food into the water, and when the first British surveyors mapped the area in 1807, John Robinson in his report commented, 'The fishes at this place are so tame as to eat out of one's hand when rice is given them and to see them scrambling and jumping over one another for food produces a pleasing sight.'

The scene is sadly changed today. Dams have been built and the water harnessed to a hydro-electric scheme. Only a small trickle now dribbles down the bare rockface and pilgrims rarely visit the site.

122

123

123 'Cape Comorin, taken near Calcad' (IV, *Twenty-four Landscapes*, 1). *See also colour plate XXVII*

August 1792. 'To the southernmost point of the peninsula of India has been given the name of Cape Comorin, and this appellation navigators have transferred to the lofty mountain situated not far distant from its extremity, which is a well known and conspicuous landmark to those who navigate the eastern coast of the peninsula. This view is taken in the vicinity of a small village called Calcad [Kalakad]; it is a place of no account, but contains an Hindoo temple of considerable dimensions. Though the hills beyond that village are high, they seem almost levelled with the plain, when compared with the lofty mountain of the Cape, rising immediately behind them.'

After a careful search today the large temple in the middle distance could not be traced and one cannot help suspecting that it was invented by Thomas Daniell: a great gateway and temple complex echoing the huge triangular mountain was essential for his composition. This print, with its subtle greys and fawns and arresting composition, is one of the finest of the Daniell aquatints.

125

124 'The Great Bull, an Hindoo Idol, at Tanjore' (II, *Oriental Scenery*, 22). *Detail: see the title-page*

125 'The Great Pagoda, Tanjore' (II, *Oriental Scenery*, 24). *See also colour plate XXVIII*

September 1792. The Brihadisvara or Rajarajesvara Temple, which stands within a walled compound, was built about AD 1000. The tall pyramidal tower of the main shrine is covered with intricate sculpture and is topped by a massive domical capstone. Also in the enclosure is a colossal statue of Shiva's bull, Nandi.

'Although this building is of a form that occurs frequently in the Deccan, it differs materially both with regard to the style of its external decoration and the form of its termination at the top. It is about two hundred feet in height [actually 58 m], and stands within an area enclosed with high walls, the top of which along their whole extent is decorated in the usual manner with bulls sacred to the divinity to whose service the temple is devoted. The red stripes observable on the lower walls denote its being in the possession of the Bramins.'

The note on *no. 124* comments that 'This statue of the sacred Bull, a celebrated idol at Tanjore, is formed of a single block of stone, sixteen feet two inches [5.4 m] in length, by twelve feet six inches [3.7 m] in height, and of a kind not to be met with but at a considerable distance from Tanjore; from which circumstance the natives are very much inclined to attribute something miraculous to the bringing of it thither; particularly as no records are yet discovered respecting the time of erecting it.'

Lord Valentia, who visited the temple in 1804, was well aware of these aquatints of 'the finest specimen of the pyramidal temple in India'. So great was Thomas Daniell's reputation for the correctness of his views that Valentia noted with surprise, 'It has been drawn by Mr Daniell with some little embellishments. The Rajah was extremely anxious that I should not request to enter it. He said, if I did not insist on it, no one else could; of course I complied with his request, but went to the door to view the bull of black granite, which Mr Daniell has also drawn, but incorrectly as to the number of pillars supporting the roof over it, and the space between each of them.' The number of pillars is in fact correct, but the space has been increased in order to show the bull more clearly. (The same device is used in *nos. 141 and 142.*).

The temple greatly impressed the British. Hodges had published a view of it in 1787, although he had been unable to visit the site himself: his print was based on a drawing by an old friend, the surveyor and astronomer Michael Topping.

127

126 'A Pavilion, belonging to an Hindoo Temple' (V, *Antiquities of India*, 21)
October 1792 or February 1793. 'This view was taken near Mavelaporam on the Coromandel coast. Most of the Hindoo Temples in the southern part of Hindoostan have attached pavilions, which in general are much decorated.

They are principally used for the purpose of receiving the idol of the Temple, on those festival days when it is thought proper to make such an exhibition for the gratification of the populace. On those occasions it is conveyed to its situation with great pomp, amidst the acclamations of the people, by whom it is received with every token of enthusiastic rapture, and after the performance of certain religious rites, it is again returned to the Temple with the same pageantry, and attended with the same frantic circumstances.'

127 'Sculptured Rocks, at Mavalipuram, on the Coast of Coromandel' (V, *Antiquities of India*, 1). *Detail: see colour plate XXIX*
October 1792 or February 1793. 'Mauveleporam lies . . . on the sea coast, and is known to mariners by the name of the Seven Pagodas.'

At the southern side of Mahabalipuram is a group of five freestanding temples, as well as a great elephant, lion and bull, all hewn out of the dark granite boulders that are found on this coastal strip. They were made at the time of the Pallava dynasty during the seventh to eighth centuries. The temples are carved to resemble *raths*, wooden cars which are the vehicles of the gods. Known as the Draupadi, Arjuna, Bhima, and Dharmaraja Raths and the Sahadeva Temple, they are richly covered with sculptures.

'This view is a representation of several Rocks, which have been wrought by the Hindoos into curious architectural forms on the outside, and in the lower part excavated for the purpose of religious worship. These rocks are of very hard, coarse granite; nevertheless, the ornamental parts appear to have been executed with a considerable degree of skill, which is very evident on the western side, being there sheltered from the corroding effect of the sea air. A Lion and an Elephant appear in the centre; the former is much larger than nature, but of inferior art of some others to be met with in the neighbourhood: the latter is about the natural size: it is well designed, and the character of the animal strongly expressed.'

128 'The Entrance of an Excavated Hindoo Temple, at Mavalipuram' (V, *Antiquities of India*, 2)

October 1792 or February 1793. 'This rock, like the former [*no. 127*], is of coarse granite; the excavation consists of one large apartment, of an oblong form, leaving a small temple attached to that side opposite the entrance. The roof is supported on the sides and front by a double range of columns, all curiously, and not inelegantly, formed of natural rock. ... To the right of this excavation the rocks are sculptured with a great variety of mythological figures, many of which are extremely well carved. On the high ground to the left are the ruins of a large structure nearly mouldered away.'

It is clear from Thomas Daniell's comment to this plate that he had no idea of the subject-matter of this now-famous carving. It depicts the myth of the origin of the Ganges, which relates how a holy ascetic, Bhagiratha, eventually persuaded the gods to let the river descend from heaven. Lest the falling water should swamp the earth, the god Shiva agreed to let it flow through his tangled hair until it spilled gently out. In the relief this moment is shown and all the gods, people and animals are watching the miracle. The sculpture has a wonderful impromptu quality, taking advantage of the great grooved rocks and plain surfaces.

< 129

130 'Western Entrance of Fort St George' (II, *Oriental Scenery*, 12) *c.January 1793*. 'Fort St George is considered by engineers as a work of very great strength. This bridge leads into the fort by the road from the governor's garden house. The business of the English at Madras is chiefly transacted within the fort; but in general the opulent have houses in the country a few miles from it, as the heat of the air within the fort, owing to the quantity of masonry and closeness of the buildings, is found very oppressive.'

Fort St George was gradually extended and strengthened over the years to meet threats from the French and the rulers of Mysore. Numerous buildings were huddled within the fortifications – Government House (*no.99*), St Mary's Church, consecrated in 1680, a lighthouse, arsenal, offices and houses. Here the colonnaded verandah of Government House rises above the Fort wall to the left and the tower of St Mary's Church, before the spire was added, can be seen to the right of the flag. It was not until after the Fourth Mysore War, when Seringapatam fell and Tipu Sultan was killed, that Madras was secure and the administrative centre could spread beyond the walls of the Fort.

129 'South East View of Fort St George, Madras' (II, *Oriental Scenery*, 7)

c.January 1793. 'This view is taken on the beach southward of the Fort of Madras; the larger building to the right of the flag-staff is the new exchange, and the higher one to the left is the church, to which a spire has been added since the taking of this view in the year 1793, when the other five views of Madras were likewise drawn. In the distance is seen part of the Madras roads; and in the foreground the sea breaking in with its usual turbulency on this coast; the only vessels in use for passing through this surge to communicate with the shipping, are called Massoola boats. They are flat bottomed, and built without iron, the planks being sewed together with line made from the outer coat of the cocoa nut.'

Madras, unlike Northern India, has a double monsoon – from the east in July to September and from the west in December. Many journals comment on the violent storms which at times wrecked ships anchored in the Roads. The heavy surf made landing a hazardous affair: it was done by means of *masula* boats, and as they approached the line of breaking surf the boatmen would leap out and carry the passengers ashore on their shoulders. There was great competition among young officers to assist in carrying attractive ladies. Messages were taken out to the ships on small catamarans, by boatmen who stowed the letters in their pointed waterproof caps.

130 >

131 'Part of the Black Town, Madras' (II, *Oriental Scenery*, 8)
c.January 1793. 'The Black Town (so called from being principally the residence of the native merchants) is distant rather less than half a mile north from Fort St George, and separated by the Esplanade; along which runs the China Bazar, or market for Chinese, India, and European merchandize. In the town the Armenians have erected a church, which appears in the distance, and to the left of it are seen the minarets of an handsome Mosque, built by Mahommed Ali, Nabob of the Carnatic.'

Indian bazaars were frequently located outside the British settlements in the interests of health. At this time little was understood about the causes of diseases such as cholera and typhoid, which frequently limited the European span of life to 'two monsoons'. They were attributed to the 'unhealthy miasmas' which emanated from the crowded bazaars. At Madras an area between the Fort and the old town which had originally been cleared as a line of fire was preserved for health reasons.

With the visit of George V the name Black Town was changed to George Town.

132 'The Amenian Bridge, near St Thomas's Mount, Madras' (II, *Oriental Scenery*, 10)
c.January 1793. 'On the road from Madras to St Thomas's Mount is the Armenian Bridge, extended over the river Meilapoor; though narrow, it is, including its causeway, four hundred and ten yards [375 m], and has twenty-nine arches, perhaps not judiciously constructed, and at present of irregular dimensions, owing to the frequent repairs it has undergone in consequence of inundations. The distant building on a eminence called the Little Mount was formerly a convent in the occupation of respectable Roman Catholics: its present inhabitants, however, though of the same faith, are few, and miserably poor.'

The road to Guindy and the southern suburbs of Madras crosses the Adyar River by the Marmalong Bridge, which has replaced the old Armenian Bridge. A Latin inscription near the north end recorded that the original structure was erected in 1726 by an Armenian, 'Petrus Usean', 'pro bono publico'.

The Little Mount in the distance is traditionally connected with the martyrdom of the Apostle St Thomas, who is supposed to have gone to India after the Crucifixion and lived there. While praying in a cave he is said to have been wounded by a Brahmin with a lance and to have then made his way to St Thomas's Mount where he died. An old church still remains but a modern one has been built beside it.

133

133 'The Assembly Rooms on the Race Ground, near Madras' (II, *Oriental Scenery*, 11)
c.January 1793. 'The Race Ground is between seven and eight miles [*c.* 12 km] from Madras, and near to St Thomas's Mount, which, in this view, appears on the the right of the Assembly Rooms. The races are supported by English gentlemen resident in Madras, and its neighbourhood. This amusement takes place in the cool season, when the ladies of the settlement are invited to a splendid ball.'

The old British military cantonment was situated south-west of Madras near St Thomas's Mount so it is not surprising that the Race Ground and Assembly Rooms were located on open ground nearby. St Thomas's Mount is crowned by a Portuguese church built in 1547 which traditionally marks the spot where St Thomas died. The hill was a favourite place of recreation for the British who would take the air there in the cool of the evening. Charlotte Florentia Clive, the little daughter of the Governor of Madras, enjoyed climbing the 132 steps that led up to the church. In February 1801 Major-General Sydenham, commander of the cantonment at the Mount, jokingly gave her a formal certificate to certify that she had accurately counted the steps during one of her evening walks.

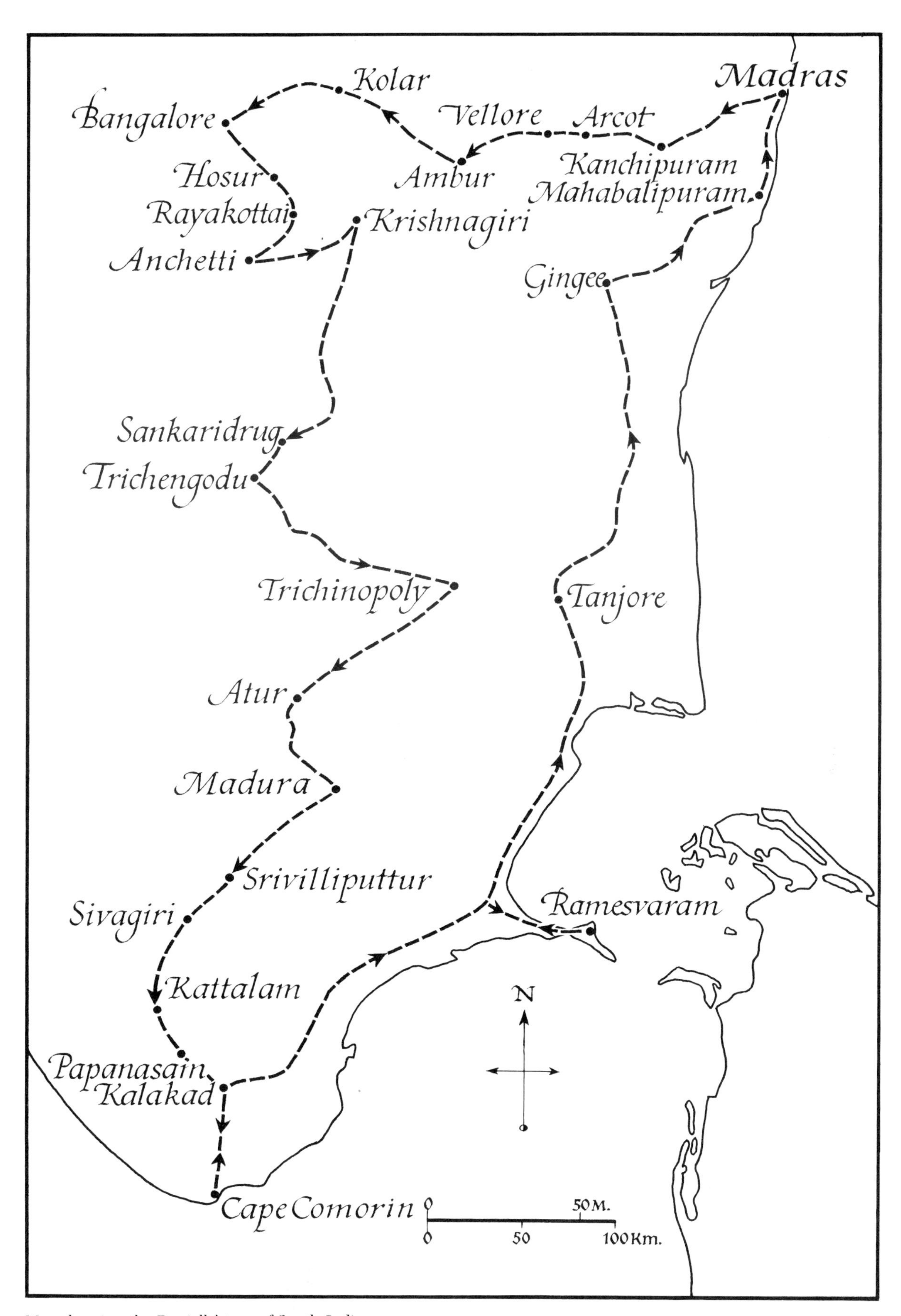

Map showing the Daniells' tour of South India.

Western India and the journey home February 1793 to September 1794

On the proceeds of the Madras lottery, the Daniells planned a final stage of their journey. By now they had spent almost seven years in India. They had visited the North and the South. In order to complete a truly grand picturesque tour they decided to travel by country boat to Bombay and spend a month or two exploring Western India. Then they would start homewards, going by sea to Muscat in Oman and continuing by the overland route through the Middle East and Europe.

They left Madras in the middle of February 1793 and reached Bombay in March, their boat having taken on stores and water at various places along the Malabar Coast. The visit to Bombay proved more stimulating than they could possibly have imagined, for they met the artist James Wales (1747–95), who had been working there since 1791. Although Wales was a portrait painter by profession, he had become wholly enthralled by the rock-cut temples of Western India. The temple of Elephanta on an island close to Bombay had long been known to Europeans, but Wales had explored many other lesser known sites around the city, as well as Karli (*nos. 144–147*) in the Western Ghats. He had found a generous patron in Sir Charles Malet, the British Resident to the court of the Maratha Peshwa at Poona. Through him Wales had not only obtained introductions to the Maratha court but had been able to visit a number of small caves near Poona such as 'Pandoo's Cave' (Panchalesvara) (*no. 142*). He was busily making drawings and measured plans with a view to publishing a lavish illustrated work on the antiquities of India when he eventually returned to England. The Daniells were delighted by his discoveries and gave him enthusiastic encouragement. With Wales as their guide they visited Elephanta and Kanheri (*nos. 134–139, XXX–XXXII*), as well as various small caves on Salsette Island, which at that time was separated from Bombay by numerous inlets of the sea. Amongst these caves was Mandapisvara, which had been partially incorporated into a Portuguese church. They also visited Jogesvari (Jugasree', *no. 141*), entered by a long passageway cut through the rock, and Kondivate ('Kondooty', *no. 140*), situated on a hillside with a superb view across to Bombay and the sea.

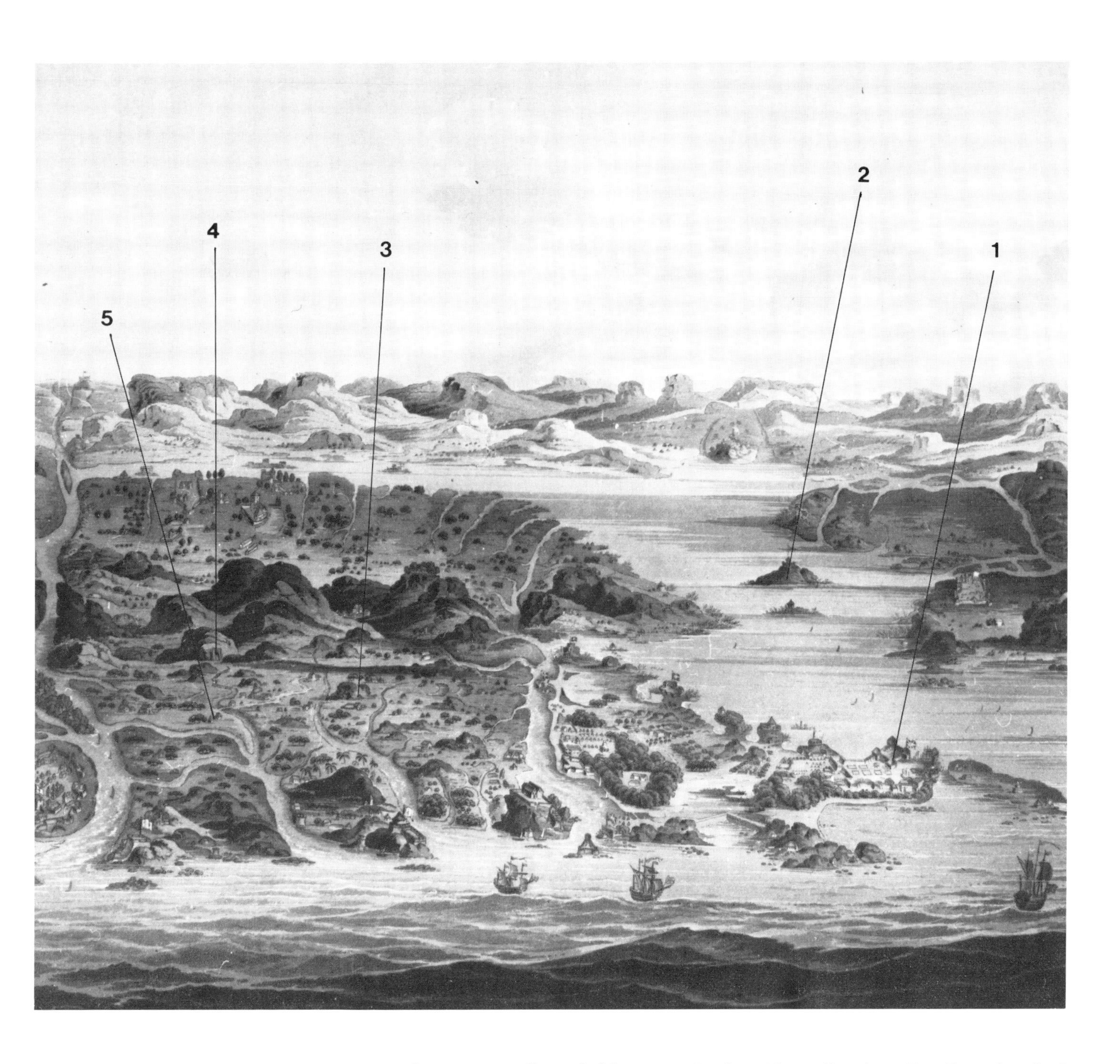

Bird's eye view of Salsette and Bombay Islands from the west, by Robert Cribb, 1803 (after a painting that belonged to Sir Charles Malet). 1 Bombay Fort, 2 Elephanta Island, 3 approximate site of Jogesvari cave, 4 entrance to Kanheri caves, 5 approximate site of Mandapisvara. (India Office Library and Records, London)

The two Daniells probably spent March to May in Bombay. By 4 June they had reached Muscat. They were no sooner there than news reached the British Factory that war had broken out in February between France and England. It was obvious that they must drop their plan of returning to England by the overland route and must return to Bombay. Thomas appears to have been officially entrusted to carry back news of the war, for much later in 1799 he informed the East India Company that he had never been paid the reward promised for this service. In Bombay the Daniells at once made contact with James Wales and by 28 July they were again sketching the caves at Kanheri. Their friendship with Wales was to prove of great significance. During the two years after the Daniells' final departure he continued his exploration of the Western caves. In February and March 1795 he visited Ellora and made numerous drawings of the Buddhist, Brahmanical and Jain caves (*nos. 149–172, XXXIII*), but eight months later, while working in the Kanheri caves, he caught fever and on 18 November 1795 he died. It was through Thomas Daniell that publicity was eventually given to his work (see p. 221).

The Daniells soon found that a passage directly back to England would be long delayed. Since the East India Company's main trade was with China it was easier to get a passage from there than from Bombay and the artists appear to have taken a country ship to Canton, arriving some time in September 1793. Once again they had to wait, but eventually they joined up with a convoy escorting Lord Macartney's embassy back to England: a group of thirteen East Indiamen together with a Spanish, a Portuguese and an American boat all sailed from Whampoa on 10 January 1794, and after journeying via the Straits of Sunda, Mauritius, the Cape of Good Hope and St Helena, the Daniells reached Spithead in September 1794. The two artists had been away from England for nine and a half years.

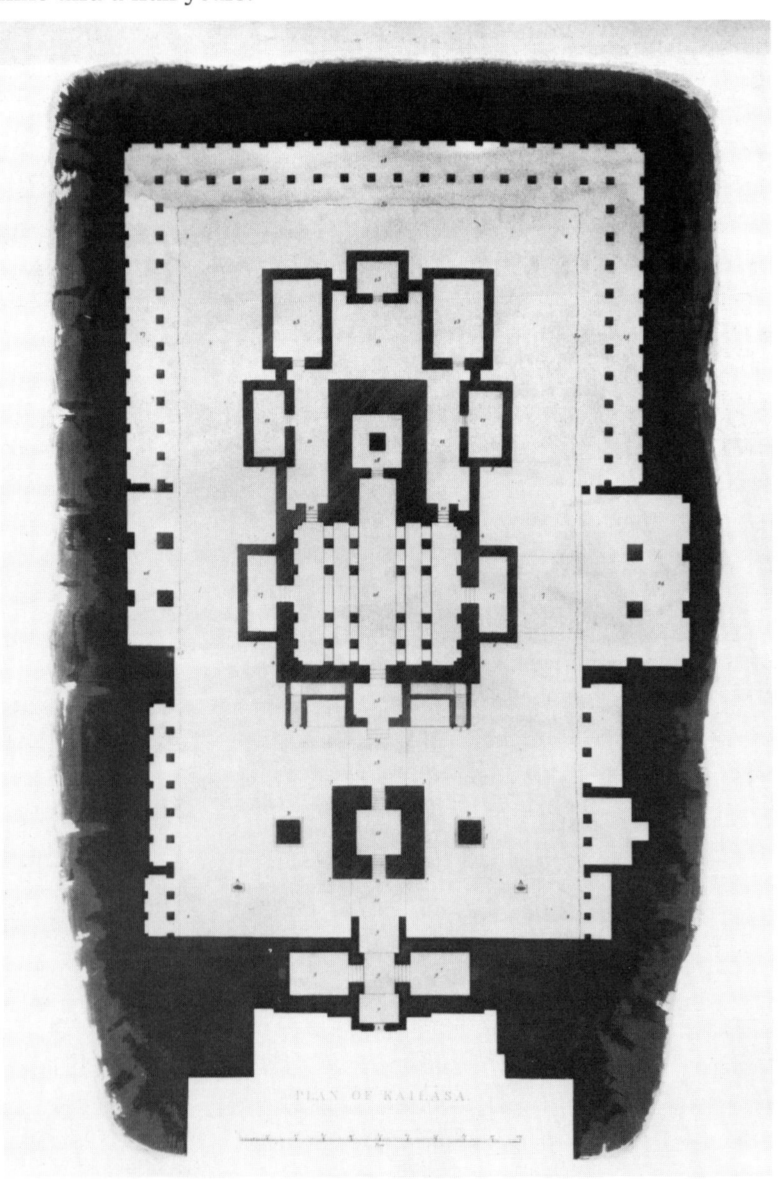

Plan of the Kailasanatha Temple at Ellora, from the Daniells' publication of Wales's drawings. Reading upwards from the bottom: entrance screen, room below the Nandi shrine with pillars on either side, assembly hall, lingam shrine surrounded by subsidiary shrines (see *nos. 161–164*). (India Office Library and Records, London)

134

134, 135 'The Entrance to the Elephanta Cave', and 'Part of the Interior of the Elephanta' (V, *Antiquities of India*, 7 and 8). *See also colour plate XXX*

c.July 1793. This cave, located as it is on an island off the entrance to Bombay harbour, had early been noticed by Europeans coming to India. A sculptured elephant that originally stood at the south end had given the island its name of Elephanta.

The view in *no. 134*, Thomas Daniell explains, 'represents the principal entrance facing the north; it has also other openings to the east and west. ... The ceiling appears originally to have been supported by thirty-two detached pillars, forming nine iles [aisles] in length, and five in breadth, exclusive of the veranda, or portico, at the entrance, and of the recess on the side opposite, containing the Trimourte, or triple-headed idol; several of the pillars however are now destroyed.'

The main shrine of the Shiva temple is situated in the centre of the cave (*no. 135*). At the four entrances stand great guardian figures. The square flat-roofed cella, surrounded by a pillared hall allowing circumambulation under cover, was a common form of temple architecture by the seventh century, but this shrine dates from the sixth.

'This excavation is considerably elevated above the sea; the floor, nevertheless, is generally covered with water during the monsoon season; the rain being then driven in by the wind.' (In fact, water drains in from the hill above.)

135

136

137

136–138 'An Excavated Temple on the Island of Salsette', 'The Portico of an Excavated Temple on the Island of Salsette', and 'The Interior of an Excavated Hindoo Temple, on the Island of Salsette' (V, *Antiquities of India*, 3, 4, 12). *See also colour plates XXXI, XXXII c.July 1795*. These three prints depict the Great Chaitya Temple (Cave 3) at Kanheri on the island of Salsette. Of the more than 100 Buddhist shrines that were carved into the rocky hill between the second century and the middle of the sixth, it is one of the earliest.

138

Thomas Daniell comments that the cave 'appears from some of the figures in the portico to have been dedicated to Booda. On each side the area, between the outer steps and the portico attached to the rock, is a large octangular pillar; on that to the right, above the capital, is a group of lions.' He goes on to describe the sculpture of 'Mahadeva, surmounted by an umbrella' and 'the Chacra of Vichnou'. His comments show how confused scholars were at the time and how difficult they found it to distinguish between Buddhist and Hindu cave-temples. This cave dates from about AD 150; the giant Buddhas were added some 350 years later.

When Lord Valentia visited the cave in 1804 he noted that the giant figures at the ends of the portico 'are in perfect preservation in consequence of their having been Christened and painted red by the Portuguese, who left them as an appendage to a Christian church, for such this temple of Boodh became under their transforming hands.'

Faced with the interior (*no. 138*), Thomas Daniell commented on the carving of the capitals, but the nature of the *dagoba* or stupa, which he called an 'idol', defeated him. James Wales, who had drawn the rock-cut temple at Karli in 1792, may well have pointed out to the Daniells the similarity between its interior (*no. 147*) and that of Kanheri. Both have columns with vase-shaped bases and capitals topped with sculptures of elephants, horses and human couples, and the stupas are similar.

139 'Part of the Kanaree Caves, Salsette' (V, *Antiquities of India*, 11) *c.July 1793*. 'This excavation appears immediately on the right hand of the entrance to the large Temple [*nos. 136–138*] . . . The sides of the recess, which contain the idol, are covered with various sculptures of Bhood figures in basso relievo: to the left of the centre, somewhat elevated, are two smaller chambers; and on the right, passing through irregular apertures, are two other chambers, containing also similar Bhood figures.' Like the Buddhas of the Great Chaitya Temple, these carvings date from about AD 500.

The European sketching in this engraving may well be James Wales, through whom the Daniells had come to know about the caves. It was on another visit to Kanheri in 1795 that he caught the fever from which he died. Captain George Millett, who was with him, wrote: 'Mr Wales fell a victim to the putrid Air we inhaled at the Caves in an unhealthy season of the year, with him I fear will be lost some valuable information which his investigating turn of mind, and very able Talents . . . would have enabled him to add to the correct drawings, and measurements, he was about to publish of those monuments of early genius, and human labour. Mr Wales died in my House at Bombay exceedingly lamented, and left a Family of five Orphan Girls.'

The Daniells were to make that publication possible (*nos. 140–172*).

139

140

140–148 These plates were all engraved by Thomas Daniell after drawings by James Wales. It appears that he was intending them for a further series of *Antiquities*, but abandoned the project (see pp. 221–22). The Daniells visited 'Kondooty' (*no. 140*), 'Jugasree' (*no. 141*) and 'Mundipishwer' (*no. 148*), but never saw 'Pandoo's Cave' (*no. 142*) or 'Ekvera' (*nos. 144–147*).

141

140 'Kondooty', after Wales
c.1793. The rock-cut temple of Kondivate, on a hill north–west of Bombay, is far more open than most and the whole interior can be seen from the entrance. Only one wall is carved – again, the sculpture dates from the late fifth or early sixth century – and the stupa is set inside a curved apse (see the plan, *no. 143*).

Today the door on the right is a ragged hole; the main figure is far more mutilated and the heads of all the others have deteriorated further. The lowest figure on the right has disappeared altogether. When I visited Kondivate I found an ascetic sitting in exactly the same position as in the engraving.

141 'Jugasree', after Wales
c. 1793. The temple of Jogesvari is now entered off a crowded bazaar.

A visitor today can at once tell why Wales chose for his viewpoint this spot in the inner hall: it is the only place where the light filters in, allowing him to see his paper, and creating a contrast of light and shade on the columns. His rendering is extremely accurate and only one distortion has been made – the distance between the second pillar from the right and the third has been exaggerated so as to reveal the square structure of the inner shrine which contains a lingam. In this respect a drawing can be more informative than a photograph.

Since Wales's time various changes have taken place: steps have been built up to the inner shrine and the guardian figures have been worn away by water filling the cave during the monsoon season. The temple is still in worship to Shiva.

xxx (135)

xxxi (136)

xxxii (137)

XXXIII (169)

142

143

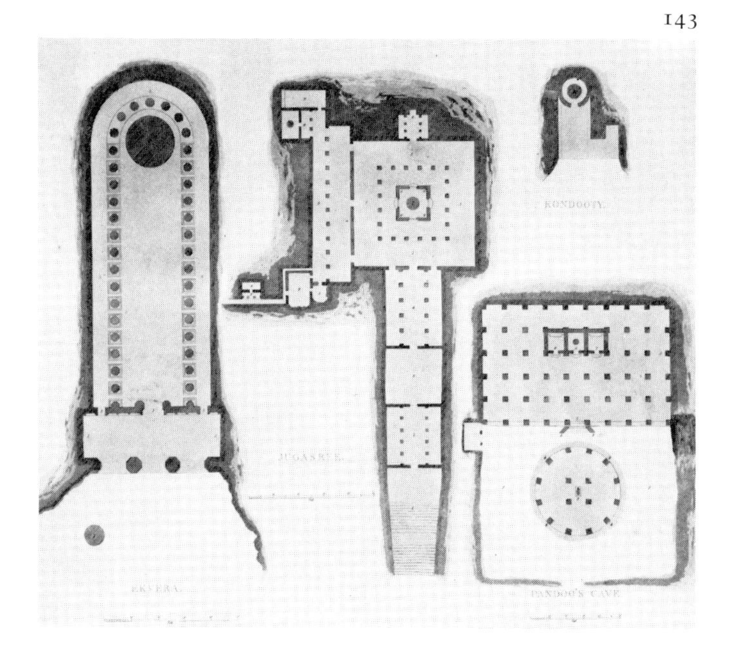

142 'Pandoo's Cave', after Wales
*c.*1792–95. This rock-cut temple near Poona is now known as Bhamburda or Panchalesvara and is still in worship. Both the central mandapam and the caves on the right have been hewn out of the same great rock (see the plan, *no.* 143). Today the water has all been drained into a cistern hollowed out from the rock in the place where the artist would have been sitting to make his drawing. In order to show the bull Nandi, in the centre, Wales has slightly distorted the position of the pillars.

James Wales's papers show that in September 1792 he sent his assistant Robert Mabon to make a drawing of 'Pandoo's Cave', but he almost certainly visited it himself later.

143 Plans of rock-cut temples, after Wales
From left to right they are 'Ekvera' (Karli, *nos.* 144–147), 'Jugasree' (Jogesvari, *no.* 141), 'Kondooty' (Kondivate, *no.* 140), and 'Pandoo's Cave' (Bhamburda or Panchalesvara, *no.* 142).

144

145

144, 145 'Ekvera', after Wales
c. 1792–95. The great rock-cut Buddhist temple of Karli, once known as 'Ekvera', lies at the top of the Western Ghats. Excavated about AD 100, it is one of the largest and most complete chaitya caves. A huge column, surmounted by a bell-shaped capital and a group of lions, stands in front; a similar pillar on the right was replaced by a small Hindu temple. The porch (see also *no. 146*) is richly carved with figures and small horseshoe-shaped 'chaitya arches'. The elephants at the sides originally had ivory tusks and metal trappings.

Wales first visited Karli in December 1792: 'Much surprised,' he noted tersely, 'being stupendous work.' He left Mabon there to draw and measure it. On a later visit he was arrested by the Maratha guard at the nearby fort of Lohgad: the motives of an English antiquary could not be understood, and he was only released when an order was received from the Peshwa's agent in Poona.

146

147

148

146, 147 'Ekvera', after Wales
A closer view of the entrance to the cave-temple of Karli (see *no. 144*), with a glimpse through to the hall; and the hall itself.

The screen is carved with figures of auspicious couples and pierced by three doors.

The great hall inside has a lofty ribbed vault 'supported' on vast octagonal columns which rest on vase-shaped bases. Above the capitals are sculptures of figures seated on kneeling elephants; similar groups on horses face the aisles. Plain pillars surround the domed stupa which is dramatically lit by a shaft of light streaming through the entrance window. The arrangement is very close to that at Kanheri (*no. 138*).

148 'Obelisks near Mundipishwer', after Wales
c.1793. Detail of an aquatint recording a group of six carved stones which in the time of Wales stood near the rock-cut shrine at Mandapisvara on the island of Salsette. The obelisks have now been moved to a site near Borivli railway station, Bombay.

Cousens, writing for the Archaeological Survey in 1931, identified them as records of a thirteenth-century conflict, described by the chronicler Hemadri, commemorating the deaths of heroes who fell in some action on land and sea, when the Yadava king Mahadeva defeated Somesvara, the Silhara king of Thana, near Bombay. 'Some of the stones shew the land battle, in which elephants, protected with coats of mail, took part, while others depict the lines of vessels, propelled with banks of oars like the old Roman biremes.' Here the upper stele shows ships, the lower one elephants.

149–171 *Hindoo Excavations in the Mountain of Ellora*
Thomas and William Daniell never visited Ellora, but Thomas engraved James Wales's drawings of the site after they had been brought back to England in 1798 by Wales's patron, Sir Charles Warre Malet. Malet himself had visited Ellora in 1793 or 1794 and had written an article on the caves in the latter year (published in *Asiatic Researches* in 1801). It was illustrated with line drawings by an Indian draughtsman, Gangaram, and Malet expressed his confidence that better drawings would be made when Wales visited the site. That visit took place in February and March 1795. Wales was accompanied by his assistant, Robert Mabon, the Indian draughtsman, Gangaram, a young Goanese painter, a carpenter, a servant, fifteen bearers and three ponies with drivers. He was planning a large publication of engravings and worked feverishly during his two months at Ellora. Thomas Daniell was to base his comments to the present plates on Malet's article, and they lack the freshness of the remarks that he made on subjects which he himself had seen.

149–151 'The Mountain of Ellora', after Wales (VI, *Hindoo Excavations in the Mountain of Ellora*, 1–3)
The rock-cut temples at Ellora extend along the face of a great rocky hill for about a mile and a quarter (some 2 km) and include 12 Buddhist, 17 Brahmanical and 5 Jain caves, in that disposition from south to north. It is in that topographical sequence, rather than in their published order, that they have been arranged here.

In this panorama Kailasa (*nos. 160–164*) is visible in the centre. The three northernmost Jain caves (*nos. 168–172*) lie outside the picture area to the left.

152 'Dehr Warra', after Wales (VI, *Hindoo Excavations in the Mountain of Ellora*, 24)
1795. Dherwara, 'The Outcasts' Quarter' (Cave 5), now known as Maharwada, is the largest of the single-storeyed viharas or monasteries and the southernmost of the Buddhist caves depicted here. Like the others (*nos. 153–156*) it probably dates from the seventh century.

'The Hallalcore's Quarter. By this designation have the Brahmans, who describe them, thought proper to discriminate this group of caves, which, though making no conspicuous figure here, would render any other place illustrious. They, under this term of pollution, endeavour to deter visitors from entering it, though the large cave is a very fine one; over the front of which a river, in the rainy season, rushes into the plain below, forming a sheet of water, that, in a beautiful cascade, covers the front of the excavation as with a curtain of crystal. There are two stripes of stone that run parallel to each other along the floor . . . and seem intended as seats either for students, scribes, or the sellers of some commodities, a convenient passage lying between them up to the Idol at the end of the cave.'

149 151

152

153

154

156

153, 154 'Viswakarma, Exterior View' and 'Viswakarma', after Wales (VI, *Hindoo Excavations in the Mountain of Ellora*, 22 and 23)
1795. 'Viswakarma is considered by the Hindoos as the artist of the gods.' Cave 10 was favoured by artisans, and is now known as the Carpenter's Cave. It is one of the most beautiful at Ellora, with galleries borne by sturdy pillars. At the top is a great projecting cornice cut out of the rock above a screen carved with flying figures.

Inside the cave in front of the stupa is a colossal Buddha, seated between two attendants beneath an arch of flying figures. Twenty-eight columns separate the nave from the aisles. The capitals are plain but above them is a long frieze of panels topped by dwarfs singing and playing musical instruments. The vault is carved with ribs to imitate a wooden structure.

'This excavation seems to possess a greater variety in the design than any other to be met with in the whole range. . . . The simplicity of the interior pillars and the large balcony in front are likewise different from any thing else to be seen in this mountain. There are two other grand excavations in this part of India, likewise with coved ceilings, but have in other respect more resemblance to each other, than either of them to this; The one is at Echvera [Karli, *no. 147*] . . . and the other on the island of Salsette [Kanheri, *no. 138*].'

155 'Dotali', after Wales (VI, *Hindoo Excavations in the Mountain of Ellora*, 21) >
1795. The 'Two-Storeyed Cave' (Cave 11) was found in 1876 to have another storey buried below, consisting of a verandah with a shrine and two cells. The simple verandahs are in strong contrast to the three cells of the middle storey which when entered are seen to be richly carved with the Buddha and Bodhisattvas.

156 'Tin-Tali', after Wales (VI, *Hindoo Excavations in the Mountain of Ellora*, 20)
1795. The lower verandah of the 'Three-Storeyed Cave' (Cave 12) opens into a great hall with three rows of columns, beyond which is yet another hall leading to the shrine with a seated Buddha on each side wall and a huge Buddha at the far end. In the middle and top storeys are further statues of the Buddha in shrines, that of the middle storey flanked by *dwarapalas* (door guardians). Like the two previous caves, 'Tin-Tali' probably dates from about AD 700.

155

157

157, 158 'The Ashes of Ravana, Interior View' and 'The Ashes of Ravana', after Wales (VI, *Hindoo Excavations in the Mountain of Ellora*, 19 and 18)

1795. From the second half of the sixth century onwards, cave-temples were excavated at Ellora by Hindu patrons (*nos. 157–167*). When Malet visited Ellora the nature and date of the caves were still uncertain, but fantasy was beginning to recede: they were the work of Hindus, he concluded, pointing out the frequency of Shiva imagery. 'The fanciful analogies of some travellers . . . now vanish: and we seek no longer for colonies of Jews, Egyptians, Ethiopians or Phoenecians' to account for their construction.

The façade of Cave 14, 'The Ashes of Ravana', had lost several of its piers, revealing the large pillared hall behind (*no. 157*), which leads to a shrine with a passage around it. The columns of the hall have capitals carved with vases and foliage. The walls are rich with sculptures showing on the south wall Shaivite subjects and on the north wall Vaishnava images, including Vishnu with his wife Lakshmi and the boar incarnation of Vishnu.

158

159 'Das Avatara', after Wales (VI, *Hindoo Excavations in the Mountain of Ellora*, 17)
1795. Cave 15, named after the ten incarnations of Vishnu, lies at the end of a courtyard cut from the rock, in the middle of which is a shrine, seen here in the foreground. The cave has two storeys – the lower one supported by plain pillars, the upper by richly carved ones.

OVERLEAF
160, 161 'The Upper Part of Kailasa', after Wales (VI, *Hindoo Excavations in the Mountain of Ellora*, 15 and 16)
1795. 'These views were taken on the rock to the right of the entrance of Kailasa, looking down on the sculptured decorations of the roofs of this magnificent temple.'

This temple is not excavated inside the rock but is actually carved out of the black volcanic hillside. Both the temple and the pillars (*no. 163*) are great lumps of stone left standing. It is estimated that some 200,000 tons must have been cut away. The temple lies, as it were, in the middle of a vast pit, over a hundred feet (30 m) deep.

This bird's-eye view, composed of two prints, brilliantly reveals the extraordinary feat represented by the Kailasanatha Temple complex, hewn from the rock in the mid- to late-eighth century. It also shows how the great outcrop of Ellora dominates the landscape (compare nos. *149–151*). Sir Charles Malet wrote, 'we are lost in wonder at the idea of forming a vast mountain into almost eternal mansions'. The motive was, he commented, 'religious zeal, the most powerful, and most universal agitator of the human mind'.

Sir James Mackintosh, Recorder of Bombay, who was normally supercilious about Indian culture, noted when he visited Ellora in 1810, 'The next is Coilas, or the "celestial mountain of silver", where Mahadeo [Shiva] resides, which beggars all description, and which, I think, must be one of the most stupendous and magnificent of the works of man. The general idea is an oblong, hollowed into the rock, leaving a mass in the centre, which has been hollowed and hewn into a pagoda. You may judge of the greatness of this work from the fact, that there are about fifty feet [*c.* 15 m] between the sides of the pagoda and the present rock. On the three sides of the rock are three stories of caves, like the boxes of a play-house.'

159

160, 161

160, 161 'The Upper Part of Kailasa', after Wales (VI, *Hindoo Excavations in the Mountain of Ellora*, 15 and 16): *see caption overleaf*

162, 163, 164 'The Entrance to Kailasa', 'S.W. View of Kailasa', and 'N.E. View of Kailasa', after Wales (VI, *Hindoo Excavations in the Mountain of Ellora*, 12, 13, 14)
1795. The Kailasanatha Temple, dedicated to Shiva, is perhaps the most impressive of the whole Ellora group (see *nos. 149–151* and the plan, p. 192). It is approached on the west side through a rock screen (*no. 162*) pierced by an entrance passage. Facing the entrance is the Nandi shrine, flanked by tall pillars which originally carried the trident of Shiva. At the centre is the great assembly hall, leading to the main lingam shrine which is surrounded by subsidiary shrines. A pillared verandah encloses the entire complex.

In *no. 163* the inside of the entrance is on the left; beyond it are the Nandi shrine (at first-floor level), a pillar, and finally the assembly hall, concealing the lingam shrine. In *no. 164* we are standing in the verandah looking back towards one of the elephants at the entrance. On the left is a subsidiary shrine, followed by the assembly hall. Their plinths are decorated with life-size elephants and lions.

Every visitor to Kailasanatha stands in wonder. E. M. Forster noted in his diary, 'Ellora, Kailas at sunset. More amazing than anything in a land where much amazes. Supporting cornice of blackened monsters – elephants, griffons and tigers who rend. The great mild face of a goddess, doing cruelty, fades into the pit-wall.'

162

163

164

< 165

167

165 'Doomar Leyna', after Wales (VI, *Hindoo Excavations in the Mountain of Ellora*, 9)
1795. Cave 29, dedicated to Shiva, is one of the largest temples cut in the later sixth century. The entrances are marked by lions with their heads turned inwards and a paw raised, and great guardian figures flank the central shrine.

166 'Rameswara', after Wales (VI, *Hindoo Excavations in the Mountain of Ellora*, 11)
1795. The cave of 'Lord Rama' (Cave 21) is a Shivaite temple with a porch in front of it.

William Hodges, although he had been unable to visit the rock-cut temples of Western India, was fascinated by the descriptions of them. For him, as for many of his generation, they were examples of 'the rude sublime' and of 'nature's colossi'. 'There is', he wrote, 'an almost universal tradition which characterises rocks and caverns as the haunts and sacred habitations of the Gods; and in consequence of which the form and gloom of such caverns have been universally imitated in the oldest temples. Their external forms and appearance is in the spiry rock, the towering cliff, and the mountain in its immense extent [*nos. 149–151*]: How varied! how grand! . . . In grottos and caverns gloom and darkness are common and desirable to both, for Fancy works best when involved in the veil of obscurity.'

167 'Junwassa', after Wales (VI, *Hindoo Excavations in the Mountain of Ellora*, 10)
1795. Sir James Mackintosh in 1810 reached this cave from 'Doomar Leyna' (*no. 165*), scrambling between the falling water of a cascade and the rock face. In 'Janoossy', 'the place of the nuptial visit', he saw 'a figure of Brama with his four heads, three of which were visible. There was also a Vishnu with a lotos, on which sat a Brama. The interior of the temple was rude and naked, which our guide explained by telling us, that Mahadeo and Parbutty [Shiva and Parvati] had come here only to be married.'

< 166

168

168, 169, 170 'The Entrance of Indra Sabha', 'View of Indra Sabha, looking outward', and 'Indra Sabha', after Wales (VI, *Hindoo Excavations in the Mountain of Ellora* 6, 7, 8). *See also colour plate XXXIII*

169

170

1795. Indra Sabha (Cave 33) is probably the earliest of the five Jain caves at Ellora (*nos. 168–172*), which date from the early ninth century and later. The temple is entered through a carved rock screen and its arrangement recalls that of Kailasanatha (*nos. 160–164*). The various chapels are filled with images of the Jain Tirthankaras or 'saints' – Parasvanath, Gomata Swami and Mahavira.

Sir Charles Malet visited Indra Sabha in 1794: 'You enter this magnificent cave, or assemblage of caves, by a handsome gateway cut from the rock, on which are two lions couchant. There is a small cave much choked before the gateway on the right hand. From the doorway, you enter an area, in which stands a pagoda, or temple of a pyramidal form in which is placed a kind of square altar, with figures on each side . . . This temple is elaborately finished with sculpture, and a mass of sculptured rock serves as the gate, left and fashioned, when the avenue to the inner apartments was cut through the stony mountain. In the same area, on the left hand side, is a very handsome obelisk, the capital of which is beautified with a group of sitting human figures that are loosened from the mass. The obelisk is fluted and ornamented with great taste, and has a very light appearance.'

No. 169 shows the view looking back towards the entrance from the main cave-temple, and *no. 170* shows that temple.

In the hillside above the entrance is another cave – 'an unfinished excavation of curious workmanship, now nearly choked up with earth.'

171

172

171 'Jagannatha Sabha', after Wales (VI, *Hindoo Excavations in the Mountain of Ellora*, 4)

1795. 'This view, which is one of the first shown to a stranger, must strike him with astonishment, whether he considers the vast labour which must have been bestowed on it in mere excavation, the rock being of red granite; or whether he considers the infinite pains which it must have taken to form the pillars and finish the numerous sculptural decorations: but when he is informed that the whole mountain is full of excavations, and that many are larger and still more elaborate, he is quite at a loss how to credit what he hears.'

The walls of this Jain temple are sculptured with figures of Parasvanath and Mahavira.

172 'Paraswa Rama Sabha', after Wales (VI, *Hindoo Excavations in the Mountain of Ellora*, 5)

1795. 'On the left hand side of the upper storey of the Indur Subba [*nos. 168–170*], there is a passage into this Subba, which though smaller than any of the foregoing, is exactly alike, and equal to them in the fabrick and preservation of its works. There is a passage from it into the upper story of Jugnath Subba [*no. 171*] . . . which will explain the contiguity of these three caves.' (Sir Charles Malet)

Parasvanath, the Jain 'saint', is represented by a great rock-cut figure in the top of the hill in which the Jain caves have been excavated.

Publication and influence

ON GETTING BACK TO ENGLAND in September 1794 the Daniells settled in London at 37 Howland Street, Fitzroy Square. They had in their possession hundreds of drawings – some mere pencil sketches, often made with the camera obscura, others wash drawings, and a number of complete watercolours suitable for the making of aquatints. The collection was comparable to the fieldwork notes of an anthropologist or travel-writer, a mass of undigested material. Most of the drawings, however, were carefully annotated with names of places and dates, lending support to the idea that when Thomas went to India in 1785 he already had in mind the eventual publication of a series of Indian views. As regards the form that this was to take he had kept an open mind and collected material of many different kinds. On returning to England he still appears to have had no clear overall plan but, with typical prudence and common sense, was prepared to sound out the market and proceed with publication step by step.

Thomas first of all planned two series, each consisting of twenty-four aquatints, entitled *Oriental Scenery: Twenty-Four Views in Hindoostan.* The first series was advertised in England on 28 March 1795.

VIEWS IN THE EAST-INDIES.

PROPOSALS for publiſhing TWENTY-FOUR VIEWS in HINDOSTAN, conſiſting of ſome of the moſt intereſting ſpecimens of ORIENTAL SCENERY; in which are repreſented many beautiful, as well as magnificent examples of the architecture of that extraordinary country, with ſuch other incidental accompaniments as have a reference to the manners and cuſtoms of its inhabitants:—from the Drawings of

Mr. THOMAS DANIELL,

Who, during a reſidence of ſeveral years in India, viſited many parts, either not at all, or but imperfectly known to Europeans. To be engraved by himſelf, and coloured in imitation of the original Drawings. The ſize of the Prints are 25 inches by 19—Price to ſubſcribers one guinea and a half the pair, to be paid for on delivery—to non-ſubſcribers two guineas. The firſt pair will be ready to be delivered on the 31ſt inſt. and a pair every two months, till the ſett is completed. Publiſhed for Mr Thomas Daniell, No. 37, Howland-ſtreet, by R. Bowyer, Hiſtoric Gallery, Pall-mall, where ſpecimens of the work may be ſeen.

Newspaper advertisement for the first series of *Oriental Scenery*, 28 March 1797. (Victoria and Albert Museum, London)

The first two plates were produced in March 1795 and Thomas sought permission to dedicate the first series to the Honourable Court of Directors of the East India Company. This was granted in May. At the same time proposals for this set were sent to India and published in the *Madras Courier* of 9 September 1795 and the *Calcutta Gazette* of 22 October. If subscribed for and delivered in India the price was to be 200 sicca rupees for a coloured set and 140 for an uncoloured set. (Very few of the latter seem to have been issued.) Half the subscription was to be paid upon delivery of the first twelve views. It was hoped that they would arrive by the earliest ships of the 1796 season. On 30 October 1796 the *Madras Courier* reported that specimens of the first series had arrived, and also announced proposals for a second series containing a further twenty-four views in four parts. The price quoted for each series was 24 guineas in England and 60 pagodas in India.

The first series, published between March 1795 and January 1797, contained views of buildings which lay on the route familiar to travellers on their journey 'up the country' by river via Patna, Maner, Benares, Chunargarh, Allahabad and Kara. These were places that had also been visited or drawn by William Hodges. Scenes of Delhi, Sikandra and Agra were included as well, since through their links with the Great Mughal they had an immediate appeal for the British. At the same time a number of the views broke new ground and reflected Thomas Daniell's own interests. They depicted buildings that were far less well-known – the Muslim fort at Rohtasgarh, Hindu temples at Agori and Gaya and the ruined city of Gaur.

The second series, also entitled *Oriental Scenery: Twenty-Four Views in Hindoostan*, was published between August 1797 and December 1798 and dedicated to the Rt Hon. Henry Dundas, President of the Board of Commissioners for the Affairs of India. It contained a very different mixture of subjects. The first two parts, each of six engravings, depicted British buildings in Calcutta and Madras. The Calcutta views acted as an appendix to the original twelve *Views of Calcutta*. It was now ten years since the latter had been published: many changes had taken place, and Thomas rightly guessed that additional views would be welcomed by Bengal Company servants. The aquatints of Madras were the first to be published by an artist who had actually visited the city. The third and fourth parts extended knowledge of Indian architecture in South India by including six views of Madura and two of Tanjore. Four views of Trichinopoly through their connection with Clive and the wars with the French had a special interest for the British.

Thomas and William worked relentlessly and managed to publish two aquatints regularly every two months. That each series had been planned as a whole is proved by the fact that the engraved plate numbers do not always correspond to the order of publication: in the second series, for example, plates VII and VIII had been produced a year before plates III–VI. By August 1799 Farington notes that Thomas Daniell had received an order from Madras for forty sets, worth about £1,200. On 17 December 1800 the *Madras Courier* announced that the first two series were complete and that a few sets 'pasted into portfolios' had been shipped to India. The popularity of the first two series of aquatints is proved by the high price which they commanded at the auction of Claud Martin's possessions in 1801, the first series selling for 270 rupees and the second for 250.

As well as producing these aquatints, between 1795 and 1798 Thomas Daniell exhibited twelve oils at the Royal Academy and William showed six. Thomas was made an A.R.A. in 1796 and R.A. in 1799. His views of Indian architecture in both oils and aquatint had begun to arouse great interest in British intellectual circles. Aware of this, between October 1799 and June 1800 he produced a set of twelve views of Indian temples and sculpture entitled *Antiquities of India*, dedicated to the Society of Antiquaries of which he had become a Fellow on 11 April 1799. This group of prints (which forms the first half of the set conventionally known as the fifth series) depicted the rock-cut temples of Elephanta and Kanheri in Western India, a Hindu temple at Deo in Bihar, and carvings on the rocks at Sultanganj on the Ganges and at Mahabalipuram in South India. Thomas was obviously indulging his own interests and enthusiasms for Indian architecture and looking to a more specialized market. Once again Hodges had forestalled him: in 1787 he had produced a treatise on architecture illustrated with two engravings of Sher Shah's mausoleum at Sasaram and one of Akbar's mausoleum at Sikandra. However Thomas Daniell in his *Antiquities* presented a far more impressive set of illustrations which recorded his own strong antiquarian leanings. The series was far more esoteric than the first two and it seems probable that the sale was not great, since he did not add a further group of twelve plates to complete a set of twenty-four until much later, in 1808.

Instead during 1801 Thomas Daniell produced two large aquatints of the Taj Mahal at Agra – one a view of the mausoleum from across the River Jumna and the other a view of it from the garden side. It seems probable that Thomas had encountered some criticism for not including a typical view of the Taj Mahal in his first publications: he had only shown the principal gate in his first series. The two lavish prints were accompanied by a booklet which described the mausoleum in laudatory terms and included a ground plan.

Encouraged by the success of the first two series, the Daniells in August 1801 set to work on another group. Again entitled *Oriental Scenery: Twenty-Four Views in Hindoostan*, it was completed in June 1803. Permission for the dedication – to the Rt Hon. George Viscount Lewisham, who had succeeded Dundas as President of the Board of Commissioners – appears to have been given in June 1801, suggesting that the whole series had been planned well in advance. Twenty of the aquatints supplemented the first series and consisted of further views of architecture, chiefly Muslim, in upper India. The views of Rajmahal, Ramnagar, Chunar, Allahabad and Kara were of monuments and places which were familiar to travellers up the Ganges. Those of Delhi, Lucknow and Faizabad also had a strong appeal for many of the British, but the views of Rohtasgarh, Kanauj, Pilibhit and Jaunpur, as well as those of the holy cities of Mathura and Gaya, were far less familiar. At the same time the Daniells took advantage of a renewed interest in Mysore and Tipu Sultan. While the artists had been busy with their second series, the Fourth Mysore War had broken out, and Tipu Sultan had been killed in May 1799 during the siege of Seringapatam. As a result the British had gained control of Mysore. Once again there was a popular curiosity about the terrain through which the British army had advanced and the Daniells were able to make use of their drawings of the great hill forts in the Baramahal Hills at Jagdeo, Rayakottai, Verapadrug and Hosur.

With the third series completed, Thomas once again broke off and returned to making aquatints of further archaeological sites. Since his return to England his friend James Wales had died (see *no. 139*), and in 1798 Wales's patron, Sir Charles Malet, had returned to England, bringing with him all the drawings of cave-temples (and also Wales's orphaned daughter, Susanna, whom he conducted to his mother's house and married in 1799). Sir Charles contacted Thomas Daniell and discussed the possibility of publishing some of Wales's material. This proposition greatly appealed to the artist and it was considered that the drawings of Ellora were the most important. Twenty-four views and eight ground plans, including a panorama of the whole site as well as views of the most important caves, were engraved 'by and under the direction of Thomas Daniell' and published on 1 June 1803 as *Hindoo Excavations in the Mountain of Ellora near Aurungabad in the Decan*. A descriptive booklet was published a year later, on 1 June 1804, and the set (now known as the sixth series) was dedicated to Sir Charles Malet who had commissioned and paid for the work.

At the same time it appears that Sir Charles and Thomas Daniell were planning a further set of twenty-four 'antiquities' depicting the sculpture of Elephanta and the lesser sites of Western India, also based on James Wales's drawings. Eight plates and a plan were published on 1 July 1803. They included views of two caves on Salsette Island, carved obelisks at Mandapisvara, 'Pandoo's Cave' near Poona, four views of Karli, and a group of ground plans relating to these temples. Very few copies appear to have been made and only one complete set, in the India Office Library, is at present known. Even in 1847 the bookseller, Henry G. Bohn, who bought up remainders, listed the set as 'very scarce' in his catalogue of books and prints: 'Daniell's (Thomas) Views and Antiquities of the Temples of Salsette, viz. Ekvera, Jugasree, Kondooty, and Pandoo's Cave, with Obelisks near Mundepishwer, 9 large plates, finely coloured, mounted on card-board, (pub. at £10.10s) very scarce, £4.4s.' He also listed 'Unpublished Plates of the Antiquities of the Temples of Elephanta and Salsette. 13 large Etchings. £3.3s.' These appear to have been mainly depictions of sculpture inside the temple of Elephanta. With two more plans they would with the former group have made up a further set of twenty-four plates. No copies of them have as yet been traced. It seems probable that the *Hindoo Excavations in the Mountain of Ellora* were not proving popular – even today they sell less well than the other series – and the first eight prints of the new set may have been even less well received. Although because of their own enthusiasm and also as an act of piety both Thomas Daniell and Sir Charles Malet would have liked to have published a second series after Wales's drawings, Malet may well have felt that it was not financially viable. Only a few copies were made and the project then halted.

Both Thomas and William Daniell continued to exhibit oil paintings regularly at the Royal Academy and the British Institution. These depicted not only monuments but also picturesque landscapes, such as the waterfall at Papanasam, mountain scenery in Garhwal and forest scenes in South India. Since 1800 Thomas Daniell had been receiving patronage from the 3rd Earl of Egremont, who invited him to Petworth in that year and again in 1805. The Earl had purchased six oils from him of 'sublime' and 'picturesque' subjects, including the temples at Trichengodu and a forest scene in Dindigul. It was clear that there was a market for views which appealed not only to those who knew India but to connoisseurs with a taste for romantic landscape and architecture. Between January 1804 and January 1805, therefore, Thomas and William produced *Twenty-Four Landscapes: Views in Hindoostan*, twelve aquatints appearing in January 1804 and two every following two months. The set, known as the fourth series, was appropriately dedicated to the Rt Hon. George O'Brien, Earl of Egremont, and the title page was dated May 1807. The plates included seven views of the hilly country of South India, ten of the Garhwal mountains near Srinagar, two near the foothills, views on the Hooghly and Ganges, two in Shahabad District, Bihar, and one at Kanauj. They made a completely new contribution to the British knowledge of India. The Himalayas, the forested area of South India with its great waterfalls, and the interior of Bihar were as yet almost unknown. This fourth series is perhaps the most magnificent of all the groups produced by the Daniells.

In the next year, 1808, Thomas returned to his favourite subject of antiquities, he and his nephew publishing a further twelve engravings of buildings. They do not appear to have been issued with any title or dedication and they are commonly linked to the twelve *Antiquities of India* published in 1799 and 1800, to form the fifth series. The subjects were varied, including Hindu temples in Bihar, a Muslim *idgah*, a tank, minarets at Delhi and Gaur, the Observatory at Delhi and various strange sculptured symbols near temples at Bangalore.

Leaving aside the two views of the Taj Mahal and the supplementary plates made from Wales's drawings, six groups had now been published, with six booklets of text to accompany the plates. The cost of the complete set was 200 guineas bound. The first series had been published by Robert Bowyer at the Historic Gallery, Pall Mall, but the remainder were all published by Thomas

Daniell himself. In 1810, however, Thomas arranged for a bookseller, Miller, to use the plates and produce a further twenty-five complete sets. Thomas agreed to refrain from selling the remainder of his sets until Miller had disposed of his, or to pay Miller a proportion of his profits. The size of the editions published by Daniell is not known but the copper plates used for aquatinting are quickly worn and the print run cannot have been large – perhaps not more than two hundred. Bohn when remaindering the work in 1847 noted that 'The complete sets are to be seldom met with, as the artists finished them only in small numbers.' Thomas Sutton had heard that the original copper plates were taken in the 1920s to India where many new prints were pulled from them, but no examples have recently been traced to confirm this suggestion.

So lavish a publication could necessarily only be purchased by the wealthy. Yet it was clear that a wider demand existed. Between 1812 and 1816, therefore, Thomas and William published a small quarto version with plates 'Reduced from their folio edition'. The plates were bound into three landscape volumes at £18.18*s.* for uncoloured and £21 for coloured copies. In 1816 another issue was published bound into one volume: the title page states that the views were 'Drawn and Engraved by Thomas and William Daniell, London. Published by the Authors, MDCCCXVI', but the plates are the same. In these two collections the views are arranged in six sections: each corresponds to one of the six series already mentioned, but the original order of publication is not followed, the two archaeological sets being placed at the end. The entire quarto edition is entitled *Oriental Scenery*, giving rise to some confusion, since of the large published sets only three had that title. Nevertheless, it is by this name and in this sequence that the Daniells' aquatints are now commonly known, and in Appendix I the plates will be found listed in this order.

Oriental Scenery was later to attract attention in France. Hodges' *Select Views* had been published with titles and text in both English and French, but the Daniells' titles and booklets were all in English. However, the great orientalist Louis Matthieu Langlès (1763–1824), who was Keeper of the Royal Library in Paris, republished in his *Monuments anciens et modernes de l'Indoustan* (1812, 1821) a number of the Daniells' aquatints, chiefly of South Indian monuments. In 1828 the Daniells, aware of the French interest in their work, approached the Asiatic Society of Paris concerning a further publication of engravings depicting 'scenery, architecture, antiquities, costumes and natural history'. The Society strongly recommended that 'Messers Daniell should be encouraged to publish a selection from their extensive and unrivalled collection of drawings', but no financial help was offered and no more was heard of the project.

After completing the *Antiquities of India* in December 1808, the Daniells produced a smaller and more popular volume in 1810 entitled *A Picturesque Voyage to India by the Way of China.* It consisted of fifty aquatints depicting the places visited by the artists on their various journeys to and from China and to India. Unlike the plates of their great work, which are about 18 by 24 inches (45 by 61 cm), these illustrations are only $4\frac{3}{4}$ by $7\frac{1}{2}$ inches (12 by 19 cm). The five views showing their approach to Calcutta and the city itself have been included here (*nos. 1–3, 16, 17*). The book contained a highly significant introduction in which Thomas Daniell summed up in a masterly manner the attitude of the Picturesque Traveller engaged on a Picturesque Tour of India:

> It was an honourable feature in the late century, that the passion for discovery, originally kindled by the thirst for gold, was exalted to higher and nobler aims than commercial speculations. Since this new era of civilisation, a liberal spirit of curiosity has prompted undertakings to which avarice lent no incentive, and fortune annexed no reward: associations have been formed, not for piracy, but humanity: science has had her adventurers, and philanthropy her achievements: the shores of Asia have been invaded by a race of students with no rapacity but for lettered relics; by naturalists, whose cruelty extends not to one human inhabitant; by philosophers, ambitious for the extirpation of error, and the diffusion of truth. It remains for the artist to claim his part in these guiltless spoliations, and to transport to Europe the picturesque beauties of those favoured regions . . . There are, perhaps, few of us who have not been impelled by stronger motives than curiosity to trace the progress of an Indian voyage; and to acquire some local ideas of those distant regions which it has been the good fortune of our friends or relatives to explore. To assist the imagination in this erratic flight is the object of the following work: delineation is the only medium by which a faithful description can be given of sensible images: the pencil is narrative to the eye; and however minute in its relations, can scarcely become tedious; its representations are not liable to the omissions of memory, or the misconceptions of fancy; whatever it communicates is a transcript of nature.

The publication of all these aquatints had been a mammoth task. The two artists prepared almost all the plates themselves. At first Thomas had the major role but as the work progressed William rapidly became expert. The engraved title-pages issued with the plates trace these changes: the first series was 'Drawn and Engraved by Thomas Daniell', and the second was '. . . from the Drawings of Thomas Daniell. Engraved by himself and William Daniell', while the third and fourth series were 'drawn and engraved by Thomas and William Daniell'. The *Antiquities of India* were made only 'from the Drawings of Thomas Daniell, R.A. & F.S.A. Engraved by himself and William Daniell' (though the individual plates attribute both drawing and engraving to both men). The *Hindoo Excavations* and the supplementary antiquities were made from the drawings of James Wales and engraved 'by and under the direction of Thomas Daniell'. The clear implication is that William cared more about people and scenery than about purely archaeological subjects. It was his uncle whose great interest lay in antiquities.

In the making of the first four series William came to play an increasingly important part. He himself was later to tell Farington that during the first seven years after their return from India he frequently worked from six in the morning till midnight. As a result of this rigorous apprenticeship he became one of the greatest aquatinters of the nineteenth century: he not only produced his own *Voyage round Great Britain* (1814–15) and many other English views but was later to work up the watercolours of many amateur artists who had lived in the East, such as Samuel Davis, Colonel Robert Smith and Captain J. Kershaw. He was able to translate a watercolour into a skilled aquatint, preserving at the same time with the greatest sensitivity the style of the original.

When aquatinting was first introduced in England reddish-brown ink was commonly used for the printing, as can be seen in certain copies of William Hodges' *Select Views*. The Daniells, however, used sepia, grey and bluish grey for printing. They usually 'stained' the prints themselves so as to reproduce the original watercolour exactly. They would normally employ colourists only to add the small touches of local colour in the figures or in clumps of vegetation in the foreground, although it is probable that the *Antiquities of India* and the prints made after the drawings of James Wales were coloured by employees under the direction of Thomas.

The superb quality of the Daniells' technique was quickly appreciated. A review written for *The British Critic* in March 1805, when all but the last twelve views of *Antiquities* had been published, is full of admiration: 'The whole is, to our taste and apprehension, as beautiful in execution, as it is possible for any views to be, which are not entirely drawings. The union of engraving with colouring cannot, we conceive, certainly will not easily, be carried to higher excellence.' 'An eminent engraver', a writer in *A Review of Fine Arts* confirmed in 1817,

> is no sinecure man; no drone in the British hive; no callous receiver of the hard-earned property of others; no mean stipendiary of a corrupt administration. His work is the efficient and fancy-delighting result of severe toil and inquisitive looking at elemental nature. In transcribing her on copper at an immense expense of time and talent, he procures the intelligent and refined portion of the community a very considerable, cheap, and elegant addition to their enjoyment.

During the late eighteenth and early nineteenth centuries many fine sets of aquatints were being produced recording the scenery of countries other than India, but amongst all these the plates of *Oriental Scenery* are probably the largest and most ambitious, as well as the most sensitive and delicate in their colouring and technique. The bookseller Henry Bohn was not making too great a claim when he noted in his catalogue of 1847: 'It is almost unnecessary to say any thing in commendation of this extraordinary work, which is, without exception, the most magnificent series of views ever produced in this, or any other country.'

The Daniells' Indian aquatints soon made an impact on the British public and on British culture at a number of different levels. They naturally had an immediate popular appeal for all who were connected with India. Company servants, whether still living there or retired to Britain, delighted in the scenes which recalled the country where they had worked. Merchants and businessmen in England who had commercial links with India, such as Charles Hampden Turner (1772–1856), enjoyed the pictures as reminders of the country with which they had such lucrative connections. They would frame the prints for their walls or purchase the great tomes for their libraries.

More important was the impact of the aquatints on sophisticated circles interested in the picturesque, the sublime and the exotic (see p. 10). The Daniells, although aware of these attitudes, were themselves simple straightforward men and in no way theorists. They were far less intellectual than William Hodges, who in his treatise on architecture, *A dissertation on the prototypes of architecture, Hindoo, Moorish and Gothic* (1787), and his *Travels in India 1780–83* (1793) had shown that he was well in line with contemporary thought. His theories were echoed in his own impressionistic aquatints, *Select Views in India* (1786–88). Buildings are depicted with violent contrasts of light and shade; they have jagged contours and are silhouetted against the sky in irregular masses. Their surface is rough and ruins are shaggy with moss and

'A most astonishing Rock rising suddenly out of the plain' near Naldurgum in South India, recorded by William in his diary for 16 May 1792, and by Thomas in this oil of a 'singular' landscape. (Inchcape & Co. Ltd)

stunted scrub. Odd-shaped rocks and bristly clumps of grass dominate the foreground and gnarled windswept trees lean across the sky. Figures and animals are unkempt and wild; the water of rivers is disturbed. There is a air of unrest which frequently communicates a frisson and shock. Hodges' engravings are in fact the epitome of the picturesque. Today his wilful distortions and vigorous compositions have a great appeal, but for his own period he was perhaps almost too extreme.

In contrast to Hodges' aquatints, those of the Daniells were stylistically far more conventional. They accorded with the principles of classical ideal landscape as seen in the work of Poussin and Claude, and it is significant that the Daniells carried with them around India Earlom's mezzotints of Claude's landscapes. Occasional concessions are made in their engravings to current fashions – a blasted tree or rough rocks – but taken as a whole their work is smooth and precise with an air of classical composure. Their landscapes include a misty blue sky, a middle distance with some feature such as a fort or pavilion to show the graduation of distance, a foreground with lively details of figures or plants, and 'side-skips' of trees or buildings which bind the whole composition together. Yet while their manner was easily acceptable, their subject-matter was frequently entirely novel and included striking elements which instantly appealed to lovers of the sublime. Here were vast waterfalls, frightening forests, towering hills, huge temples, mosques and palaces, gigantic carvings and dark rock-cut caves. At times strange rocks or religious symbols (*no. 102*), as well as towers and buildings of unusual shape (*nos. 40, 92*), dominate the scene through their 'singularity'. Here was a medley of romantic, picturesque, sublime, and exotic Indian elements which were quite unfamiliar to the British.

Thomas Daniell made numerous careful jottings of architectural details. They provided him with information when working up watercolours and aquatints, and from them Cockerell and Repton learned authentic Indian motifs. (India Office Library and Records, London)

At the same time the Daniells' aquatints also provided new and stimulating material for those who were attracted by cultures other than the Graeco-Roman. Interest in the traditions and history of regions outside Western Europe had been growing rapidly, and folios of prints depicting not only Greece and Sicily but also Egypt, the Middle East, China, and the South Seas were being produced. In this context the Daniells' views were of the greatest importance. They were 'pure' landscape, for unlike scenes of Italy or Greece they were devoid of literary associations; and they offered the first detailed representation of Hindu and Muslim architecture. Both artists were still working in the topographical tradition and would frequently use the camera obscura when drawing an intricate building. Although Hodges once again had a far more intellectual and perspicacious enthusiasm for Indian architecture, his engravings provided far less factual information for scholars and connoisseurs. It is significant to compare scenes which Hodges and the Daniells both drew from a similar angle – the entrance to a mosque at Chunargarh (*no. 69*), the Atala Mosque at Jaunpur (*no. 73*), and the mausoleum at Makhdam Shah Daulat at Maner (*no. 22*). Hodges' picturesque approach, which merged the architecture into the landscape and exaggerated certain qualities, inevitably distorted architectural forms and conveyed little detail (see p. 99). The Daniells, on the other hand, were meticulously precise and correct. The *Monthly Magazine* summed up contemporary opinion:

> The execution of these drawings is indeed masterly; there is every reason to confide in the fidelity of the representations; and the effect produced by this rich and splendid display of oriental scenery is truly striking. Every thing is

Thomas Daniell's 'Composition', painted for Thomas Hope (Private collection), and Hope's illustration of his Indian Room (from *Household Furniture and Interior Design*, 1807), showing the painting on the right-hand wall and two other oils by Thomas Daniell at the far end of the room.

drawn with the most astonishing accuracy. The animals, trees, and plants, are studies for the naturalist. The views were taken by Mr. Daniell, with singular perseverence and industry, during a long residence in India.

Altogether, *Oriental Scenery* added greatly to the knowledge of India and at the same time popularized the Indian style by giving it picturesque associations. As a contemporary reviewer in *The British Critic* wrote, 'The plates are at once a profound study for the architect or antiquary and a source of delight to the lover of the picturesque.'

For cultured men like the 3rd Earl of Egremont (1751–1837), Sir Richard Colt Hoare (1758–1838) and Thomas Hope (1769–1831), all patrons of the Daniells, *Oriental Scenery* opened up new vistas. It is not surprising that Thomas Hope, when endeavouring to stress the importance of traditions other than the classical, turned to the work of the Daniells. In the Indian or Blue Drawing Room at his Duchess Street mansion in London he was attempting to synthesize Greek, Egyptian, Turkish and Indian motifs. At the end of his book, *Household Furniture* (1807), he listed the works that had been of use to him in his 'attempt to animate the different pieces of furniture here described, and to give each a peculiar countenance and character, a pleasing outline, and an appropriate meaning'. Amongst these works, which included Stuart's publications on Athens, Denon's on Egypt, Wood's on Palmyra and Baalbec and Howell's on Sicily, were 'Daniell's Indian Views'. The eclectic approach to the picturesque was symbolized by a painting which Hope commissioned from Thomas Daniell, probably in 1799, as a companion to Panini's view of ruins in Rome which hung in the Indian Room. Entitled *Large Composition of Architecture representing some of the most celebrated Hindoo and Moorish Buildings in India*, it brought together on a single canvas various images selected from

Staffordshire earthenware transfer-printed with motifs from *Oriental Scenery*, *c.* 1810–20: a meat dish, probably by Rogers, a plate by J. & R. Riley, and a jug. (Private collection)

Thomas's travels – the Taj Mahal (*no.* 29), a South Indian temple gateway at Trichengodu, the trident of Shiva and quoit of Vishnu (*no.* 102) – and linked them into one surrealist fantasy.

This new approach to the world's cultures found a light-hearted and popular expression in the decorative arts. Here too *Oriental Scenery* played a crucial role.

In the field of ceramics, Staffordshire blue-and-white pottery in the early years of the nineteenth century was frequently decorated with topographical scenes taken from books of engravings. English country houses, views on the Continent, in Asia Minor and America all appear on plates, jugs and dishes. Not surprisingly, around the years 1810–1820 scenes of India taken from *Oriental Scenery* were added to this repertoire. The firm of John and George Rogers of Longport (*c.* 1784–1842) and J. & R. Riley of Burslem (*c.* 1802–28) specialized in such work. Sometimes the designs kept close to the original prints, but frequently they were concocted with gay abandon from several different engravings. That on the meat dish illustrated here is very similar to the print, 'Remains of an Ancient Building near Firoz Shah's Cotilla, Delhi' (*no.* 42), but a banyan tree droops its roots across the sky and English lilies, primroses and daisies burgeon round the rim. A plate made by J. & R. Riley combines two comically unrelated prints: a house in the bazaar taken from 'View on the Chitpore Road, Calcutta' (*no.* 98) is set beside 'The Sacred Tree of the Hindoos at Gyah, Bahar' (*no.* 88), while a group of indeterminate gentlemen stand in the foreground. Auriculas, violets and foxgloves cluster around the edge. The jug is an even more intricate jigsaw. The building on one side is formed from three different prints: the dome is based on that of the mausoleum of Makhdam Shah Daulat at Maner (*no.* 22), while the steps and gate are from 'View in the Fort, Madura' (*no.* 115) and drawn in reverse. On the other side of the jug is a scene of figures enlarged from those in the foreground of the 'Eastern gate of the Jummah Musjid at Delhi' (*no.* 35), and below is a building similar to that on the top of the rock of Trichinopoly (*no.* 110). Around the rim are little mosques and palm trees. Many other examples of Staffordshire blue-and-white pottery can be found which naively unite unrelated details selected from a wide range of aquatints in *Oriental Scenery*. Taken as a whole these wares did much to contribute to the popular romantic view of India which flourished in the early years of the nineteenth century.

Another field where the Daniells' engravings made their appearance was in the design of wallpapers. From the last decade of the eighteenth century French manufacturers had begun to print scenic papers, the strips of which, stretching from cornice to chair rail, formed a continuous panorama round the wall of a room. Twenty to thirty widths were frequently used. The vogue for these 'paysages' or 'paysages décors' continued until about 1840. As with Staffordshire pottery, a fashion arose for panoramas using details selected from the great illustrated travel books of the day. The first firm to produce a paper of this type was Jean Zuber of Rixheim near Mulhouse, Haut-Rhin, with his *Vues de Suisse* (1804). In the same year the firm of Joseph Dufour at Macon produced a panorama designed by J. C. Charvet consisting of twenty strips entitled *Voyages du Capitaine Cook.* The firm moved to Paris in 1807.

Although no engravings from *Oriental Scenery* were published in France until 1812, it is clear that the work was well known, for in 1806 it provided Zuber with material for a panoramic paper entitled *L'Indoustan.* This consisted of twenty strips, and used eighty-five colours and 1,265 wood blocks for the hand-

Part of a panoramic wallpaper produced by Zuber of Rixheim, 1806. The motifs in this paper also include subjects from Hodges' *Select Views*: a tower of the Katra at Murshidabad, as drawn by him, appears here in the background to the left of the fishing nets. (Deutsches Tapetenmuseum, Kassel)

printing. It was probably the work of Zuber's chief designer, Mongin (1761–1827). Examples of this paper are rare but there is a set in the Deutsches Tapetenmuseum at Kassel in West Germany.

In 1815 Dufour followed suit with *Paysage Indien* or *Vues de l'Inde*, which also included details from *Oriental Scenery*. Portions of this paper are still at Laxton Hall in Northamptonshire, a Neo-Classical house built by Humphry Repton and his son, John Adey Repton, in 1805–11. It has been suggested that George Dance who added the hall of the house in 1812 may have been responsible for introducing this paper, but in view of Humphry Repton's close connection with Thomas Daniell (see below) it is possible that the choice was his.

As with the Staffordshire potters, the wallpaper designers took details at random from *Oriental Scenery* and arranged them in a haphazard manner to form a continuous design. In Zuber's paper wild ascetics sit in front of the great statue of the bull, Nandi, at the Brihadisvara Temple at Tanjore (panel 14; *no. 124*). Beside them is a broken piece of sculpture carved with a detail in miniature from the 'Descent of the Ganges' relief at Mahabalipuram (*no. 28*). The mausoleum of Makhdam Shah Daulat (*no. 22*) rises from a river on which a country boat taken from 'Near Currah, on the River Ganges' (*no. 26*) sails past. 'View in the Fort, Madura' (*no. 115*) appears in another panel beside two fisherfolk who stand in front of tents taken from the 'Palace of Nawaub Suja Dowla, at Lucnow' (*no. 60*). In the distance is the rock at Sultanganj (*no. 89*). These varied motifs are intermixed with exotic vegetation of tropical luxuriance.

The Dufour wallpaper also includes a number of monuments taken from plates in *Oriental Scenery* – the temples at Brindaban (*no. 32*), the 'View in the Fort, Madura' (*no. 115*) and the rock of Trichinopoly (*no. 110*). Against these backgrounds appear lively groups of figures and animals unrelated to the Daniell prints: a leopard is attacked as it climbs a tree, mounted horsemen gallop after a tiger, a prince goes hunting on an elephant, a party of Europeans watch a nautch.

Detail of a panel from Dufour's scenic wallpaper, *Paysage Indien*, 1815, showing one of the temples at Brindaban (*no. 32*). (Whitworth Art Gallery, University of Manchester)

The temple/memorial to Warren Hastings at Melchet Park, from an aquatint drawn and engraved by William Daniell, 1802. (India Office Library and Records, London)

In a pamphlet published in 1804–05 to accompany the Captain Cook wallpaper, Dufour expressed the hope that it would 'assist in creating by means of new comparisons, a community of taste and enjoyment between those who live in a state of civilisation and those who are at the outset of the use of their native intelligence'. In a similar way *Oriental Scenery* played its part in creating these 'new comparisons' and a new 'community of taste and enjoyment'.

Of far greater significance was the influence of the Daniells' engravings on architecture, which led during the first quarter of the nineteenth century to an Indian phase. Hodges' work had already had a modest effect in this sphere. It was to his *Select Views* that Sir Joshua Reynolds was referring when in his XIIIth Discourse to the Royal Academy on 11 December 1786 he hoped that the views published by 'a member of this Academy' might furnish architects 'not with Models to copy, but with hints of composition and general effect which would not otherwise have occurred'. It was also Hodges' work which probably influenced George Dance in his 1788 plans for the London Guildhall and his later work at Cole Orton, Stratton Park, Norman Place and Ashburnham. Dance and Hodges were well acquainted and in 1788 had sat on the Royal Academy Council together. It also seems likely that Hodges' engravings had influenced his friend Samuel Pepys Cockerell when he was designing Daylesford House for Warren Hastings between 1790 and 1793. The Indian-type finial on the shallow dome is similar to the one that Hodges had admired on the tomb of Makhdam Shah Daulat at Maner.

Thomas Daniell's influence, however, was to be greater than that of Hodges, for his meticulous depiction of Indian architecture provided architects with far more accurate detail. This was first seen when he was invited by Major John Osborne to design a garden folly for his house at Melchet Park in Hampshire. Osborne was an unconventional character who had served in the Bengal Army, and had been court-martialled in 1771 for 'unmannerly, unmilitary and disrespectful behaviour'. He later entered the service of the Nawab of Oudh and had retired to England by 1787. Disgusted by the trial of Warren Hastings, he decided to raise a temple in his garden to contain a bust of the great man, honouring him as an incarnation of the Hindu deity Vishnu, 'who, according to the belief of the Brahmans, has from time to time appeared under various material forms for the support of religion and virtue and the reformation of mankind'. Thomas Daniell designed the folly in the form of a little Hindu temple based on the porch of the temple in the fort of Rohtasgarh (*no. 82*). William Daniell published an engraving of the building about 1802 which stated that the work was carried out by C. F. Rossi to a design 'furnished gratuitously by Mr Thomas Daniell Esq. after the chastest models of Hindu architecture'. Two bulls, the vehicle of Shiva, crown the porch and the elephant-headed god of 'wisdom and policy' adorns the entrance. He later published two plates of the temple for the *European Magazine* of December 1802.

In about 1805 Sir Charles Cockerell (1755–1836), a Bengal civil servant who had retired from India in 1800, decided to build a house for himself in Indian style at Sezincote in the Cotswolds. He had known the Daniells in Calcutta when he was Paymaster General. As architect he chose his younger brother, Samuel Pepys Cockerell. Humphry Repton, who was already a leading figure in the stylistic revolution against the classical style, was invited to design the garden and Thomas Daniell was asked to give his advice to both experts. The first result was the house, with Muslim style onion domes, multi-foil arches,

Sezincote. *Right*, the conservatory and house, designed by S. P. Cockerell, painted by Thomas Daniell in 1817 (Private collection). *Below*, the arch above the front door. *Bottom*, the bridge by Thomas Daniell.

corner pavilions (*chhatris*) and deep bracket cornices (*chujjas*) which bear a close resemblance to detail on buildings such as the Lal Bagh at Faizabad (*no.* 59). Thomas Daniell himself designed the farm buildings and dairy with a Muslim gateway and minarets, as well as the garden ornaments. By 1811 he was busy designing a bridge with Hindu pillars embellished with four small statues of the bull, Nandi. Above the pool he planned a little temple enshrining a statue of the sun-god Surya, and in the centre of the pool was a fountain in the form of a Shiva lingam. When the whole project was finished Sir Charles Cockerell commissioned Thomas Daniell to paint a set of six oils of the estate which were exhibited at the Royal Academy in 1818 and 1819. In 1817 John Martin had published ten prints of Sezincote and there seems little doubt that this link with the Daniells and their prints later influenced his own vast architectural scenes such as *Belshazzar's Feast*. Similarly Joseph Gandy's great fantasies probably owe much to the Daniells' work.

Oriental Scenery was to have further important repercussions on English architecture. In about 1803 the Prince Regent commissioned a Royal Stables and a Riding House at Brighton and the work was given to a relatively little-known architect, William Porden (*c.* 1755–1822). The Stables, built between 1803 and 1808, as well as the great Dome of the Riding House which was designed a few years later, showed strong Indian influence. There is little doubt that Porden, who had worked in the office of S. P. Cockerell, had also been influenced by the work of Thomas Daniell. As early as 1797, indeed, he had exhibited at the Royal Academy 'a design for a place of amusement in the style of the Mahometan architecture of Hindostan'.

It also happened that about 1805, when Repton was discussing plans for Sezincote with Sir Charles Cockerell, the Prince Regent was contemplating the rebuilding of his Marine Pavilion at Brighton. This had been built by Henry Holland in 1778 but was proving far too small. The Prince was not entirely satisfied with the Chinese designs for an extension which Holland had submitted and he commissioned Repton to produce alternative plans. Through the collaboration with Thomas Daniell over Sezincote, Repton had been deeply influenced by drawings and aquatints of India: he admitted that when he was first consulted by Cockerell the subject of Indian architecture was entirely new to him; but now, he observed in *An Enquiry into the Changes of Taste in Landscape Gardening and Architecture* (1806),

Plate from Repton's *Designs for the Pavillon at Brighton*, 1808. On the far left are the private apartments (compare *no. 37*); above the trees just to the right of the Pavilion is the aviary (see *no. 32*); other Indian motifs appear not only in the Pavillion itself but in the surrounding walls and kiosks. Porden's Dome appears on the right. (Victoria and Albert Museum, London)

> I cannot suppress my opinion that we are on the eve of some great future change in both these arts [Gardening and Architecture] in consequence of our having lately become acquainted with Scenery and Buildings in the interior provinces of India. The beautiful designs published by Daniell, Hodges and other artists, have produced a new source of beauty, of elegance and grace, which may justly vie with the best specimens of Grecian and Gothic architecture.

When Repton saw Daniell's drawings and prints

> a new field opened itself; and as I became more acquainted with them . . . I was pleased at having discovered new sources of beauty and variety, which might gratify that thirst for novelty, so dangerous to good taste in any system long established; because it is much safer to depart entirely from any given style, than to admit changes and modifications in its proportions, that tend to destroy its character.

'I should recommend', he continued,

> the use of such Indian forms or proportions, as bear the least resemblance to those either of the Grecian or Gothic style, with which they are liable to be compared. If the pillars resemble Grecian Columns, or if the apertures resemble Gothic Arches, they will offend, by seeming to be incorrect specimens of well known forms, and create a mixed style, as disgusting to the classic observer, as the mixture in Queen Elizabeth's Gothic. But if, from the best models of Indian Structures, such parts only be selected as cannot be compared with any known style of English Buildings, even those whom novelty cannot delight, will have little cause to regret the introduction of new beauties.

Detail of John Martin's small mezzotint of *Belshazzar's Feast*, after his painting of 1820. The heavy pillars show the influence of Thomas Daniell's aquatints of the rock-cut temples of Western India. (British Museum, London)

Full of enthusiasm for Sezincote, Repton in 1806 produced drawings for the Prince Regent which included details closely related to a number of the Daniell aquatints. The octagon which terminated the private apartments was borrowed from the bastion of Shahjahanabad as depicted in the 'View of the Cotsea Bhaug' (*no. 37*). The small gateway of the western gardens was inspired by the little temple in the Rohtasgarh Fort (*no. 82*). The aviary design was a witty interpretation of the aquatint 'Hindoo Temples at Bindrabund' (*no. 32*) and Thomas Daniell's Academy Diploma work of 1797. The turret of the

pheasantry resembles those crowning the pavilion at Allahabad (*no. 64*). Repton's interior scheme for the Brighton Pavilion included heavy pillars and vaulting reminiscent of the cave temples at Elephanta, Kanheri and Ellora. His designs were published as a folio of aquatints in 1808 and included acknowledgments to 'my ingenious friend Mr T. Daniell'.

The carrying out of Repton's plans proved impossible, as the Prince Regent had spent far too much on the Dome. For his Pavilion he eventually turned to John Nash, whose designs were realized in 1815–22. Nash was no purist like Repton: he was happy to create a fantasy of onion domes, minarets and fretwork colonnades distilled from *Oriental Scenery*. Although the architecture provides no direct link with individual aquatints, Nash's knowledge of the Daniells' work is confirmed by Farington, who mentions that in September 1818 the architect had borrowed four volumes of *Oriental Scenery* from the Royal Library at Carlton House.

The influence of *Oriental Scenery* on British architecture continued for a number of years and extended over a wide area. In Brighton several houses and civic buildings, as well as the Sassoon Mausoleum, have Indian allusions. The Mount Zion Baptist Chapel at Devonport in Devon and the Clifton Baths at Gravesend in Kent show the same idioms, and Cheltenham in Gloucestershire, where many 'Anglo-Indians' retired, had its own Indian-influenced architecture: the entrance to the New Market House, which was built by a local architect, Edward Jenkins, and completed in 1823, had three cusped arches and Indian-style crenellations and turrets. The garden of the Earl of Shrewsbury's house, Alton Towers in Staffordshire, contained an excavated Indian cave-temple. Pattern books for villas, such as Edmund Aiken's *Designs for villas and other rural buildings* (1808), frequently included houses 'in the Eastern style'. One of the most striking, depicted by Robert Lugar in his *Architectural sketches for cottages, rural dwellings and villas* (1805), is based on the 'Mausoleum of Sultan Purveiz, near Allahabad' (*no. 68*). Ireland also had buildings which were strongly Indian in their design – the lodge gateway at Dromana in County Waterford (1826, rebuilt in the 1840s) and the mausoleum of the Stephenson family (who had connections with India) at Kilbride, Co. Antrim, the latter clearly based on a Mughal tomb. Through their aquatints Thomas and William Daniell undoubtedly made a significant contribution to that elegant synthesis of styles which characterized the Late Georgian period.

The Clifton Baths, Gravesend, designed in 1830 possibly by Amon Henry Wilds (and now demolished), included 'Muslim' arches and roofs and heavy columns recalling cave-temple architecture. (National Monuments Record)

Thomas Daniell was to live for many years after the publication of *Oriental Scenery* and the *Picturesque Voyage to India*. Unlike William, who developed his own career as a painter and engraver of areas other than India, Thomas remained devoted to the country which had affected and fertilized his whole life. His style changed little over the years and he made few concessions to changing fashions. The numerous oils that he continued to produce, based on his Indian drawings, served to reinforce the impact of the aquatints. But of all his work it was *Oriental Scenery* that played a crucial role in forming the British view of India. It naturalized the landscape and monuments of India and distilled a romantic vision of that country which has been absorbed to become a part of British life and culture. Even today, after years of political and administrative links, the popular vision of India still remains that created by *Oriental Scenery*. As a contemporary admirer wrote of that great work, 'The East was clearly reflected as the moon in a lake.'

Appendix 1

Prints by the Daniells after their own Indian drawings

Views of Calcutta

12 coloured aquatints, engraved surface $15\frac{3}{4} \times 20\frac{1}{4}$ in. (40×51.4 cm). Issued without margins or titles. At the lower corner of each plate the inscription: 'T. Daniell, fecit, Calcutta', with serial number and date. 1786–88.

Oriental Scenery

In Six Parts, 144 coloured aquatints and 6 uncoloured engraved title pages, engraved surface variable, *c.* 18×24 in. (45×61 cm).
6 parts, large folio, 1795–1808. Published at £210.
An 8vo volume of text issued with each part, the title page and the titles of the prints there differing in minor details from the engraved titles.

I Engraved title: **Oriental Scenery**: Twenty-Four Views in Hindoostan, taken in the years 1789 and 1790; Drawn and Engraved by Thomas Daniell, and, with permission, respectfully dedicated to the Honourable Court of Directors of the East India Company, London, March 1, 1795.
Plates inscribed: Drawn and Engraved by Thomas Daniell [and serial number]. Published as the Act Directs for Thos. Daniell by Robt. Bowyer at the Historic Gallery, Pall Mall [and date].

1 Eastern Gate of the Jummah Musjid at Delhi *March 1795*
2 Hindoo Temples at Bindrabund on the River Jumna *March 1795*
3 North East View of the Cotsea Bhaug, on the River Jumna, Delhi *May 1795*
4 Ruins at the Antient City of Gour formerly on the Banks of the River Ganges *May 1795*
5 Raje Gaut, the Principal Road up to Rotas Ghur, Bahar *July 1795*
6 The Chalees Satoon in the Fort of Allahabad on the River Jumna *July 1795*
7 Remains of an Ancient Building near Firoz Shah's Cotilla, Delhi *Sept. 1795*
8 Part of the Palace in the Fort of Allahabad *Sept. 1795*
9 Gate of the Tomb of the Emperor Akbar at Secundra, near Agra *Nov. 1795*
10 Part of the City of Patna, on the River Ganges *Nov. 1795*
11 An Antient Hindoo Temple, in the Fort of Rotas, Bahar *Jan. 1796*
12 The Mausoleum of Mucdoom Shah Dowlut, at Moneah, on the River Soane *Jan. 1796*
13 The Western Entrance of Shere Shah's Fort, Delhi *March 1796*
14 Ramnugur near Benares on the Ganges *March 1796*
15 The Sacred Tree of the Hindoos at Gyah, Bahar *May 1796*
16 Dusasumade Gaut, at Bernares, on the Ganges *May 1796*
17 Mausoleum of Sultan Chusero, near Allahabad *July 1796*
18 The Taje Mahel, at Agra *July 1796*
19 Hindoo Temples at Agouree, on the River Soane, Bahar *Sept. 1796*
20 N.W. View of Rotas Ghur, Bahar *Sept. 1796*
21 Near Currah, on the River Ganges *Nov. 1796*
22 Mausoleum of Sultan Purveiz, near Allahabad *Nov. 1796*
23 The Jummah Musjed, Delhi *Jan. 1797*
24 Gate leading to a Musjed, at Chunar Ghur *Jan. 1797*

II Engraved title: **Oriental Scenery**: Twenty-four Views in Hindoostan [taken in the year 1792]; Drawn by Thomas Daniell and engraved by himself and William Daniell; and with permission respectfully dedicated to the Right Honourable Henry Dundas, one of His Majesty's Principal Secretaries of State, President of the Board of Commissioners for the Affairs of India, Treasurer of the Navy, &c., &c., &c., London, August, 1797.
Plates inscribed: Drawn by Thos. Daniell, Engraved by Thos. & Wm. Daniell [and serial number]. Published as the Act directs by Thos. Daniell, Howland Street, Fitzroy Square [and date].

1 View taken on the Esplanade, Calcutta *Aug. 1797*
2 View on the Chitpore Road, Calcutta *Aug. 1797*
3 The Council House, Calcutta *Feb. 1798*
4 The Writers' Buildings, Calcutta *Feb. 1798*
5 Govinda Ram Mittee's Pagoda, Calcutta *Aug. 1798*
6 Part of Cheringhee, Calcutta *Aug. 1798*
7 South East View of Fort St George, Madras *Sept. 1797*
8 Part of the Black Town, Madras *Sept. 1797*
9 The Government House, Fort St George, Madras *March 1798*
10 The Armenian Bridge, near St Thomas's Mount, Madras *March 1798*
11 The Assembly Rooms on the Race Ground, near Madras *Sept. 1798*
12 Western Entrance of Fort St George *Sept. 1798*
13 Part of the Palace, Madura *Nov. 1797*
14 View in the Fort, Madura *Nov. 1797*
15 Interior View of the Palace, Madura *May 1798*
16 An Hindoo Temple, at Madura *May 1798*
17 Ruins of the Palace, Madura *Nov. 1798*
18 Tremal Naig's Choultry, Madura *Nov. 1798*
19 The Rock of Tritchinopoly, taken on the River Cauvery *Dec. 1797*
20 The Great Pagoda, Tritchinopoly *Dec. 1797*
21 View in the Fort of Tritchinopoly *July 1798*
22 The Great Bull, an Hindoo Idol, at Tanjore *July 1798*
23 South East View of Tritchinopoly *Dec. 1798*
24 The Great Pagoda, Tanjore *Dec. 1798*

III Engraved title: **Oriental Scenery**: Twenty-four Views in Hindoostan, Drawn and engraved by Thomas and William Daniell, and, with permission, respectfully dedicated to the Right Honourable George Viscount Lewisham, President of the Board of Commissioners for the Affairs of India, London, June, 1801.
Plates inscribed as in Series Two, but 'Drawn & Engraved by Thos. & Wm. Daniell.'

1 Near the Fort of Currah, on the River Ganges *1 Aug. 1801*
2 Ruins in Rotas Gur, Bahar *1 Aug. 1801*
3 Gate of the Loll-Baug, at Fyzabad *1 Oct. 1801*
4 Mausoleum of the Ranee, Wife of the Emperor Jehangir, near Allahabad *1 Oct 1801*
5 The Punj Mahalla Gate, Lucnow *1 Dec. 1801*
6 The Mausoleum of Amir Khusero, at the Ancient City of Delhi *1 Dec. 1801*
7 Ruins at Cannouge *1 Feb. 1802*
8 The Entrance to the Mausoleums in Sultan Khusero's Garden, near Allahabad *1 Feb. 1802*
9 A Mosque at Juanpore *1 April 1802*
10 Gate of a Mosque built by Hafiz Ramut, Pillibeat *1 April 1802*
11 Jag Deo & Warrangur, Hill Forts in the Barramah'l *1 June 1802*
12 Ryacotta, in the Barramah'l *1 June 1802*
13 Verapadroog, in the Barramah'l *1 Aug. 1802*
14 Ousoor, in the Mysore *1 Aug. 1802*
15 View of Gyah, an Hindoo Town, in Bahar *1 Oct. 1802*
16 Palace of Nawaub Suja Dowla, at Lucnow *1 Oct. 1802*
17 Lucnow taken from the opposite bank of the River Goomty *1 Dec. 1802*
18 A Baolee near the Old City of Delhi *1 Dec. 1802*
19 View at Delhi, near the Mausoleum of Humaioon *1 Feb. 1803*
20 The Baolee at Ramnagur *1 Feb. 1803*
21 View from the Ruins of the Fort of Currah, on the River Ganges *1 April 1803*
22 View of Mutura, on the River Jumna *1 April 1803*
23 Mausoleum of Kausim Solemanee, at Chunar Gur *1 June 1803*
24 Mausoleum of Nawaub Asoph Khan, Rajemahel *1 June 1803*

IV Engraved title: **Twenty-Four Landscapes.** Views in Hindoostan. Drawn and engraved by Thomas & William Daniell. With permission respectfully dedicated to the Right Honourable George O'Brien, Earl of Egremont, London, May, 1807.
Plates inscribed as in Series Three.

1 Cape Comorin, taken near Calcad *1 Jan. 1804*
2 Waterfall at Puppanassum, in the Tinnevelly District *1 Jan. 1804*
3 Waterfall at Courtallum, in the Tinnevelly District *1 Jan. 1804*
4 Shevagurry *1 Jan. 1804*
5 Chevalpettore *1 Jan. 1804*
6 Near Attoor, in the Dindigul District *1 Jan. 1804*
7 Sankry Droog *1 Jan. 1804*
8 Near Bandell on the River Hoogly *1 Jan. 1804*
9 Siccra Gulley on the Ganges *1 Jan. 1804*
10 Ramgur *1 Jan. 1804*
11 Dhuah Koonde *1 Jan. 1804*
12 Cannoge, on the River Ganges *1 Jan. 1804*
13 View at Nijeibabad, near the Coaduwar Gaut *1 March 1804*
14 Coaduwar Gaut *1 March 1804*
15 View in the Koah Nulla *1 May 1804*
16 Jugeanor, in the Mountains of Sirinagur *1 May 1804*
17 View near Daramundi, in the Mountains of Sirinagur *1 July 1804*
18 Near Dusa, in the Mountains of Sirinagur *1 July 1804*
19 Buddell, opposite Bilkate in the Mountains of Sirinagur *1 Sept. 1804*
20 View on the Ram-Gunga, between Buddell and Bilkate *1 Sept. 1804*
21 View taken between Natan & Taka Ca Munda *1 Nov. 1804*
22 Between Taka Ca Munda and Sirinagur *1 Nov. 1804*
23 The Rope Bridge at Sirinagur *1 Jan. 1805*
24 View taken near the City of Sirinagur *1 Jan. 1805*

V Engraved title: **Antiquities of India.** Twelve (Twenty-four) Views from the Drawings of Thomas Daniell, R.A. & F.S.A. Engraved by himself and William Daniell. [Taken in the Years 1790 and 1793.] Dedicated respectfully to the Society of Antiquaries of London, London, Oct. 15, 1799. Printed by T. Bensley, Bolt Court, Fleet Street, 1799.
Issued in two parts, 1799–1808.
Plates inscribed as in Series Three.

1 Sculptured Rocks at Mavalipuram, on the Coast of Coromandel *15 Oct. 1799*
2 The Entrance of an Excavated Hindoo Temple, at Mavalipuram *15 Oct. 1799*
3 An Excavated Temple on the Island of Salsette *1 Dec. 1799*
4 The Portico of an Excavated Temple on the Island of Salsette *1 Dec. 1799*
5 An Hindoo Temple, at Deo, in Bahar *15 Jan. 1800*
6 Part of the Interior of an Hindoo Temple, at Deo, in Bahar *15 Jan. 1800*
7 The Entrance to the Elephanta Cave *1 March 1800*
8 Part of the Interior of the Elephanta *1 March 1800*
9 S.W. View of the Fakeer's Rock in the River Ganges, near Sultaungunge *15 April 1800*
10 S.E. View of the Fakeer's Rock in the River Ganges, near Sultaungunge *15 April 1800*
11 Part of the Kanaree Caves, Salsette *1 June 1800*
12 The Interior of an Excavated Hindoo Temple, on the island of Salsette *1 June 1800*
13 The Temple of Mandeswara near Chaynpore, Bahar *1 Dec. 1808*
14 An Antique Reservoir near Colar, in the Mysore *1 Dec. 1808*
15 Exterior of an Eed-gah near Chaynpore, Bahar *1 Dec. 1808*
16 Interior of a Temple, near Muddunpore *1 Dec. 1808*
17 View near Bangalore *1 Dec. 1808*
18 Entrance to an Hindoo Temple, near Bangalore *1 Dec. 1808*
19 The Observatory at Delhi *1 Dec. 1808*
20 The Observatory at Delhi *1 Dec. 1808*
21 A Pavilion, belonging to an Hindoo Temple [*upright*] *1 Dec. 1808*
22 Interior of the Temple of Mandeswara near Chaynpore, Bahar [*upright*] *1 Dec. 1808*
23 A Minar at Gour [*upright*] *1 Dec. 1808*
24 The Cuttub Minar, near Delhi [*upright*] *1 Dec. 1808*

VI Engraved title: **Hindoo Excavations** in the Mountain of Ellora near Aurungabad in the Decan, in Twenty-Four Views. Respectfully dedicated to Sir Charles Warre Malet, Bart., Late the British Resident at Poonah. Engraved from the Drawings of James Wales, By and Under the Direction of Thomas Daniell, London, June 1, 1803.
Plates inscribed: Drawn by James Wales. Engraved by and under the direction of Thos. Daniell – then as in Part Three [but all dated June 1, 1803].

1 The Mountain of Ellora (First View)
2 The Mountain of Ellora (Second View)
3 The Mountain of Ellora (Third View)
4 Jagannatha Sabha
5 Paraswa Rama Sabha
6 The Entrance of Indra Sabha
7 View of Indra Sabha, looking outward
8 Indra Sabha
9 Doomar Leyna
10 Junwassa
11 Rameswara
12 The Entrance to Kailasa
13 S.W. View of Kailasa
14 N.E. View of Kailasa
15 The Upper Part of Kailasa
16 The Upper Part of Kailasa
17 Das Avatara
18 The Ashes of Ravana
19 The Ashes of Ravana, Interior View
20 Tin-Tali
21 Dotali
22 Viswakarma, Exterior View
23 Viswakarma
24 Dehr Warra

ANOTHER EDITION
Oriental Scenery. One Hundred and Fifty Views of the Architecture, Antiquities and Landscape Scenery of Hindoostan. Drawn and Engraved by Thomas and William Daniell. Reduced from their folio edition . . . and carefully copied under their direction. London, printed for Thomas and William Daniell, No. 9 Cleveland Street, Fitzroy Square, and Longman, Hurst, Rees, Orme and Brown, Paternoster Row, January 1, 1812 [–1816].
6 parts, small oblong folio.
144 uncoloured aquatints, engraved surface $6\frac{1}{2} \times 9$ in. (16.5 × 22.9 cm), inscribed: Published by Thos. & Willm. Daniell, No. 9 Cleveland Street, Fitzroy Square, London, and dated from 1812 to 1816.
6 engraved titles dated as follows:

Series One. January 1, 1812
Series Two. July 1, 1812
Series Three. May 1, 1814
Series Four. May 1, 1814
Series Five. June 1, 1815
Hindoo Excavations. No date (plates dated February 1, 1816)

Text: Introduction (1 p.) in first part only, + 1 leaf of text to each plate.
Published (usually bound in 3 volumes) at £18 18*s*.: coloured copies at £21.

Another Issue **Oriental Scenery.** One Hundred and Fifty Views of the Architecture, Antiquities and Landscape Scenery of Hindoostan. Drawn and Engraved by Thomas and William Daniell. London, Published by the Authors, MDCCCXVI.
6 parts bound in 1 volume, small folio.
This is a reissue of the smaller *Oriental Scenery*, the plates being identical in every way.
Title-page differs as above.
No Introductory page.

[Antiquities of India]

8 views and one plan, inscribed: Drawn by James Wales. Engraved by and under the direction of Thos Daniell. Published as the Act directs by Thos Daniell RA. Howland Street, Fitzroy Square, London. July 1, 1803.
No title page, engraved surface $16\frac{3}{4} \times 23\frac{1}{2}$ in. (42.5 × 59.7 cm).

1 Kondooty
2 Pandoo's Cave
3 Jugasree
4 Obelisks near Mundipishwar
5 Ekvera exterior
6 Ekvera pillar and porch
7 Ekvera porch
8 Ekvera interior
9 Plans of the four cave-temples
Probably intended as another part of *Antiquities of India*. Only a very few sets appear to have been produced.

(Prints by the Daniells after their own Indian drawings, continued)

The Taje Mahal at Agra

Coloured aquatints, $21 \times 34\frac{1}{2}$ in. (53.3×87.6 cm).
Published with a descriptive booklet.
Views of the Taje Mahal at the City of Agra, in Hindoostan, Taken in 1789, 8vo, 1801.
Title as above (v. blank except for imprint: T. Bensley, Printer, Bolt Court Fleet-Street), pp. 4–7 (v. blank).
Grey paper wrappers, stitched.
With folding line-engraved ground plan by James Newton.

1 The Taje Mahel, Agra
2 The Taje Mahel, Agra. Taken in the Garden

Quarterdeck of an Indiaman

Coloured aquatint, $4\frac{1}{8} \times 7\frac{1}{4}$ in (10.5×18.4 cm).
Drawn and Engraved by Thos. & Willm. Daniell. Published by Messrs. Longman, Hurst, Rees & Orme, Paternoster Row, Feby. 1st, 1810.

A Picturesque Voyage to India by the Way of China, by Thomas Daniell, R.A., and William Daniell, A.R.A. 1810.
50 coloured aquatints, engraved surface $4\frac{3}{4} \times 7\frac{1}{2}$ in. (12.1×19 cm). Each marked 'Drawn & Engraved by Thos. & Willm. Daniell. Published by Messrs. Longman, Hurst, Rees & Orme, Paternoster Row' [and date].
Title (v. blank) + Introduction 2 pp. 1 leaf of text to each plate.
Small oblong folio, published by Longman, Hurst, Rees and Orme, Paternoster Row, and William Daniell, No 9 Cleveland Street, Fitzroy Square. 1810. Published at £12 12*s.*

Interesting Selection from Animated Nature with Illustrative Scenery; designed and engraved by William Daniell, A.R.A., London; Printd (sic) for T. Cadell and W. Davies, Strand, London; by G. Sidney, Northumberland Street, Strand, no date [1807–12].
2 volumes, oblong folio, boards, $10\frac{3}{4} \times 15$ in. (27.3×38 cm). Title (verso blank) List of Subjects (verso blank) and one leaf of text to each plate.
120 aquatint engravings, engraved surface $6 \times 8\frac{3}{8}$ in. (15.2×22.2 cm), each bearing inscription 'Designed and Engraved by Willm. Daniell & Published by Messrs. Cadell & Davies, London' [and date]. Published at £15 15*s.* (but *London Catalogue of Books* . . ., 1800–1827, says £10 10*s.*).
Some engravings have Indian landscapes as backgrounds to animals, birds, insects, fish, trees and plants.

Appendix II

Prints by other artists after the Daniells' Indian pictures

Pennant, T. **The View of Hindoostan,** 2 volumes, 4to, 1798.
Etchings on copper by T. W. Tomkins after Thomas Daniell, engraved surface $5\frac{3}{4} \times 6\frac{3}{4}$ in. (14.6×17.1 cm).

Volume I
Frontispiece: A Pandaram/A Yogey, T. Daniell, pinxt.

Volume II
Frontispiece: An Aged Brahmin/A Young Brahmin/A Ghossain Faquir, T. Daniell, pinxt.
Plate 4: A Bengalese Woman/A Tamulian man and woman, T. Daniell, pinxt.
Plate 5: A Rohilla/A Polygar/A Soldier of Tippoo's, T. Daniell, pinxt.

Twenty-Four Views in Hindostan Drawn by William Orme from the Original Pictures Painted by Mr. [Thomas] Daniell and Colonel [Francis Swain] Ward. Folio. London, Edward Orme, 1805. Sometimes bound with F. W. Blagdon, *A brief history of ancient and modern India.*
Coloured aquatints, engraved surface as below.
The following after Thomas Daniell:

Distant View of Mootee Thurna, engraved by—Fellows *Jan. 1802* $11\frac{7}{8} \times 16\frac{7}{8}$ in. (30.2×42.8 cm)
West Gate of Firoz Shah's Cotilla, Delhi, engraved by—Fellows *Jan. 1802* $12 \times 16\frac{3}{4}$ in. (30.5×42.5 cm)
The Tomb of a Moorish Lady, Bengal, engraved by J. C. Stadler *1 Jan. 1803* $11\frac{3}{4} \times 16\frac{1}{8}$ in. (29.8×41 cm)
Thebet Mountains, engraved by H. Merke *1 Jan. 1804* $11\frac{5}{8} \times 16\frac{1}{2}$ in. (29.5×41.9 cm)
The Bridge at Juonpore, Bengal, engraved by H. Merke *21 July 1804* $11\frac{3}{4} \times 16\frac{1}{8}$ in. (29.8×41 cm)
A Pagoda, engraved by J. C. Stadler *30 July 1804* $12 \times 16\frac{7}{8}$ in. (30.5×42.8 cm)
A Hindoo Place of Worship, engraved by J. C. Stadler *30 July 1804* $12 \times 16\frac{3}{4}$ in. (30.5×42.5 cm)
Dalmow on the Ganges, engraved by J. C. Stadler *30 July 1804* $11\frac{7}{8} \times 17\frac{3}{8}$ in. (30.2×44 cm)
A View of Ossoore, engraved by J. C. Stadler *30 July 1804* $11\frac{3}{4} \times 16\frac{5}{8}$ in. (29.8×42.2 cm)
Felicity Hall, near Moorshedabad, Bengal, engraved by—Harraden *March 1804* $11\frac{3}{8} \times 16\frac{3}{8}$ (29.5×41.7 cm)
The paintings were in the possession of Richard Chase, Mayor of Madras, to whom the work is dedicated.

Sir C. W. Malet, Bart, the British Resident at the Court of Poonah in the Year 1790, concluding at Treaty in the Durbar with Souac Madarow, the Peshwa or Prince of the Mahratta Empire.
Mezzotint (uncoloured), $23\frac{3}{4} \times 35$ in. (60.3×88.9 cm).
Painted by T. Daniell, R.A., Engraved by Charles Turner, London, Published by R. Cribb, 14 March 1807.

Langles, L. **Monuments Anciens et Modernes de L'Hindoustan,** 4to., Paris, 1821.
Volume II contains 24 engravings, varying from $6\frac{1}{8}$ and $6\frac{1}{2} \times 8\frac{3}{4}$ in. and $8\frac{7}{8}$ in. ($15.5/16.5 \times 22.2/22.5$ cm), each plate bearing name of etcher and engraver and 'Daniell delineavit'.

Forget Me Not, 1829.
Plate at p. 127, India, View of Ganges, engraved on steel by E. Finden after Wm. Daniell, $2\frac{5}{8} \times 4$ in. (6.7×10.2 cm).

Forget Me Not, 1830.
Plate at p. 381, The Ghaut, engraved on steel, by E. Finden after Wm. Daniell, $2\frac{3}{4} \times 4$ in. (7×10.2 cm).

The Oriental Annual; or Scenes in India. 7 vols., 8vo, 1834–40. Containing 132 engravings on steel, after Original Drawings by William Daniell, R.A., and a Descriptive Account by the Rev. Hobart Caunter, B.D., [who is ghosting for William Daniell and adding from his own experiences].

Published at £1 1s. per volume, Large Paper Copies £2 12s. 6d. per volume.

These small plates (the engraved surface is $5\frac{3}{4} \times 3\frac{3}{4}$ in. (14.6 × 9.5 cm)) were made by various craftsmen, the chief of whom were Cochrane, Brandard, Reddaway, Stephenson, Cousen, Cooke, Garner, Armytage, Bourne, Allen, and Higham.

Volume I Published by Edward Bull, 1834. 22 engravings.

A Hindoo Female [*frontispiece*]
The Cuttub Minar [*vignette title*]
Setting in of the Monsoon at Madras
Temple at Mahabalipoor
Raje Gur, Gingee
Hindoo Temples at Tritchencore
Choultry at Ramiseram
Cape Comorin
Cataract at Puppanassum
Wild Elephants
Talipat Tree
Alligator and Dead Elephant
Queen of Candy
Mausoleum at Raje Mah'l
Banks of the Ganges
Mausoleum of the Emperor Shere Shah
Mosque at Benares
Shuwallah Gaut at Benares
Hill Fort at Bidzee Gur
The Banyan Tree
The Taje Mah'l at Agra
The Caparisoned Elephant
The Hirkarrah Camel
Mahadagee Scindia
The Principal Gaut at Hurdwar

Volume II Published by Bull and Churton, 1835. 22 engravings.

Interior of a Mosque, Juanpore [*frontispiece*]
Indian Fruit-seller [*vignette title*]
Rhinoceros
Yak of Tibet
The Salaam
At Nujibabad, Rohilcund
Favourite of the Harem
Mausoleum of Sufter Jung
The Agra Gate, Chauter Serai
Mosque at Muttra
The Moah-Punkee at Lucnow
Mausoleum at Lucnow
The Rajpootni Bride
Garden of the Palace, Lucnow
The Bernar Pagoda, Benares
The Kutwhuttea Gate, Rotas Gur
Temple at Muddunpore, Bahar
Great Temple at Bode Gyah
Mosque in the Coimbatore
Kutwallee Gate, Gour
Calcutta, from Garden-House Reach
Boa Constrictor and Boat's Crew

Reprinted by Bohn in 1846 in similar binding, but bearing the title *Daniell's Scenes in India.*

Volume III Published by Edward Churton, 1836. 22 engravings.

In the Harbour of Mascat [*frontispiece*]
The Adjutant [*vignette title*]
A Rich Mahomedan
The Tiger Hunt
The Choultry of Tremal Naig at Madura
Hindoo Temple at Tritchengur
The Braminee Bull
A Hindoo Woman
On the Baliapatam River
Scene near the Coast of Malabar
The Small Deer of Ceylon
Lion and Buffaloe
The Monkey and Crows
Near Mascat
The Forts of Jellali and Merani, Mascat
Bombay
Tomb of a Patan Chief, Old Delhi
Tombs of Patan Chiefs, Old Delhi
On the island of Elephanta
Entrance to the Large Cave, Salsette
The Upper Caves, Salsette

Volume IV Published by Charles Tilt, 1837. 22 engravings.

The general descriptive notes are abandoned in this volume which is subtitled 'Lives of the Moghul Emperors. By the Rev. Hobart Caunter, B.D.'

Sultan Baber [*frontispiece*]
The Fan-Leaf Palm [*vignette title*]
Crossing a Torrent in Bootan
Capta Castle, Bootan
A Mahommedan Fakeer
View near Wandepore
Mausoleum of Toghluk Shah
Palace at Tassisudon, Bootan
The Palace at Wandechy, Bootan
The Fire-Pheasant of Java
State Prison at Delhi
The Alligator and Ox
A Mogul Trooper
The Hunting Cheetah
A Mohammedan at Prayers
Patan Tomb at Toghlukabad, Old Delhi
Bridge at Old Delhi
Boats on the Ganges
Shahjehanabad
The North Gate, Old Delhi
The Bore Rushing up the Hoogley

'The views in Boutan . . . were made from sketches by the late Samuel Davis, Esq. . . . an accomplished draughtsman, with whom Mr. Daniell was personally acquainted.'—*Preface.*

Volume V Published by Charles Tilt, 1838. 22 engravings. (Title as Volumes I–III.)

Futtepore Sicri [*frontispiece*]
Hindoo Female at the Tomb of Her Child [*vignette title*]
Tomb of Baber
Houses of Patan Chiefs at Old Delhi
Deserted Mansions at Old Delhi
The Porcupine
A Mohammedan Lady presenting her Lord with a Rose
The Emperor Humayoon
Mausoleum of Humayoon
Akbar
Minar at Futtepore Sicri
Boulee at Allahabad
Part of Oude
Elephant Fighting
A Malabar Hindoo
The Fort at Juanpore
Peasant of Ceylon
Chunar Ghur
Mausoleum of Nizam-ud-Deen Oulea
Rope-Bridge at Serinagur
Guard-House at Tassisudon [*after S. Davis*]
Castle of Ponaka [*after S. Davis*]

Volume VI **Caunter's and Daniell's Oriental Annual, 1839**
Eastern Legends by the Rev. Hobart Caunter, B.D., with Twenty-two Engravings from Drawings by the Late William Daniell, R.A.
Cr. 8vo.
Published by Whittaker & Co., 1838.

Hindoo Maidens' Floating Lamps [*frontispiece*]
Brahminee Girls at a Ghaut [*vignette title*]
Entrance to the Largest Cave of Kenaree, Salsette
Boa Constrictor seizing a Government Messenger
Boats off the Malabar Coast
A Mountain Village
The Mountain Pass
Mountain Scene in the North of India
Bridge Over a Gully
Hindoo Temple at Gyah, Bahar
Loomno, looking towards Tassisudon [*after S. Davis*]
Ruins at Old Delhi
A Celebrated Well at Lucnow
Stags Fighting
Entrance to Abdallah Mirza's Country House
Women at the Well
Leopard and Bear
Grand Entrance to a Serai
Scene in the Garden of Abdallah Mirza's Palace
Patan Buildings on the Plains of Delhi
The Aubdaur, or Water-Cooler
Entrance to Abdallah Mirza's Palace at Chandahar [*after S. Davis*]

GILBERT, LINNEY. **India Illustrated**; an Historical and Descriptive Account of that Important and Interesting Country. With Numerous Splendid Steel Engravings. After Drawings by William Daniell, Esq., R.A. London: Published for the Proprietor, and Sold by the Booksellers of Calcutta, Madras, Bombay, etc., etc. No date (*c.* 1838).

BAXTER, GEORGE. Colour Prints by George Baxter after William Daniell:
Chalees Satoon (the 'Small') $3\frac{5}{8} \times 2\frac{1}{4}$ in. (9.2 × 5.7 cm). 1848
Chalees Satoon (the 'Large') $4\frac{5}{8} \times 3\frac{1}{8}$ in. (11.7 × 7.9 cm). 1850

Bibliography

ANON. Review of *Oriental Scenery*, in *The British Critic*, March 1805

ANNESLEY G. (LORD VALENTIA) *Voyages and travels to India, Ceylon, The Red Sea, Abyssinia and Egypt in 1802–1806*, 3 vols., London, 1809

ARCHER, MICHAEL 'Indian themes in English pottery', *Apollo*, August 1970, pp. 114–23

ARCHER, MILDRED 'The Daniells in India and their influence on British architecture', *Journal of the Royal Institute of British Architects*, September 1960, pp. 439–44

——'India, revealed: sketches by the Daniells', *Apollo*, November 1962, pp. 689–92

——*The Daniells in India, 1786–1793*, exhibition catalogue, Smithsonian Institution, Washington, 1962

——*Indian architecture and the British*, R.I.B.A. Drawings Series, London, 1968

——*British drawings in the India Office Library*, 2 vols., London, 1969

——*Artist adventurers in eighteenth-century India: Thomas and William Daniell*, exhibition catalogue, Spink & Son Ltd, London, 1974

——*India and British Portraiture*, London, 1979

BELLEW, CAPTAIN *Memoirs of a Griffin, or a cadet's first year in India*, London, 1843

CONNER, P. *Oriental architecture in the West*, London, 1979

COOPER, N. 'Indian architecture in England, 1780–1830', *Apollo*, August 1970, pp. 124–33

COUSENS, H. *Mediaeval temples of the Dakhan*, Archaeological Survey of India, XLV III, Imperial Series, Calcutta, 1931, pp. 20–21, pl. XV

DANIELL, W. (after DAVIS, S.) *Views of Bootan*, London, 1813

EDEN, E. *Up the country* (*ed.* E. J. Thompson), London, 1930; re-issued 1937

ELMES, J. (*ed.*) 'Catalogue of the work of English artists in the collection of Thomas Hope. Esq', *Annals of the Fine Arts for MDCCCXIX*, IV, 1820, pp. 93–97

FORBES, J. *Oriental memoirs*, 4 vols., London, 1813; 3 vols., London, 1834

FOSTER, W. 'William Hodges, R.A., in India', *Bengal past and present*, XXX, July–December 1925, pp. 1–8

——'British artists in India, 1760–1820', *The Walpole Society*, XIX, 1931, pp. 1–88

HARDIE, M. and CLAYTON, M. 'Thomas and William Daniell: their life and work', *Walker's Quarterly*, 1932, nos. 35–36, pp. 1–106

HEBER, R. *Narrative of a journey through the upper provinces of India from Calcutta to Bombay, 1824–1825*, 2 vols., London, 1828

HICKEY, W. *Memoirs* (*ed.* A. Spencer), London, 1913–25

——*Memoirs of William Hickey* (*ed.* P. Quennell), London, 1960

HODGES, W. *Select views in India, 1780–83*, London, 1785–88

——*A dissertation on the prototypes of architecture, Hindoo, Moorish and Gothic*, London, 1787

HOME, R. *Select views in Mysore*, London, 1794

HOPE, THOMAS *Household furniture and interior design executed from designs by Thomas Hope*, London, 1807

HUNTER, W. 'Astronomical observations made in the upper parts of Hindostan, and on a journey thence to Ougein', *Asiatic Researches*, IV, 1799, pp. 141–58

——'Some account of the astronomical labours of Jayasinha, raja of Ambhere, or Jayanagar', *Asiatic Researches*, V, pp. 177–211

HUSSEY, C. *The Picturesque*, London, 1927

HUXLEY, A. *Jesting Pilate*, London, 1926

LEWIS, R. J. *E. M. Forster's Passages to India*, New York, 1979

MACKINTOSH, SIR J. *Life of the Right Hon. Sir James Mackintosh* (*ed.* R. J. Mackintosh), 2 vols., London, 1835

MALET, SIR C. W. 'Description of the caves or excavations, on the mountain, about a mile to the eastward of the town of Ellora', *Asiatic Researches*, VI, 1801, pp. 389–423

MITTER, P. *Much maligned monsters. A history of European reactions to Indian art*, Oxford, 1977

MUNDY, G. C. *Pen and pencil sketches*, 2 vols., London, 1832

MUSGRAVE, C. *The Royal Pavilion, an episode in the Romantic*, 2nd ed. (rev.), 1959

NILSSON, S. *European architecture in India: 1750–1850*, London, 1969

PARKS, F. *The wanderings of a pilgrim in search of the picturesque during twenty four years in the east*, 2 vols., London, 1850

REPTON, H. *Designs for the Pavillon at Brighton*, London, 1808

——*An Enquiry into the changes of taste in landscape gardening and architecture*, London, 1806

——*Fragments on the theory and practice of landscape gardening*, London, 1816

ROBERTS, E. *Scenes and characteristics of Hindostan with sketches of Anglo-Indian society*, 3 vols., London, 1835

ROHATGI, P. 'The India Office Library's Prints of Calcutta', *Annual Report, 1972–3, India Office Library*, London, 1975, pp. 7–24

SHELLIM, M. (foreword by Mildred Archer), *India and the Daniells*, London, 1979

SKINNER, T. *Excursions in India*, 2 vols., London, 1832

STAFFORD, B. M. 'Rude sublime: the taste for nature's colossi during the late eighteenth and early nineteenth centuries', *Gazette des Beaux-Arts*, April 1976, pp. 113–26

——'Towards romantic landscape perception: illustrated travels and the rise of "singularity" as an aesthetic conception', *Art Quarterly*, I, no. 1, 1977, pp. 89–124

STEUBE, I. 'William Hodges and Warren Hastings: a study in eighteenth-century patronage', *Burlington Magazine*, October 1973, pp. 659–66

STROUD, D. *Humphry Repton*, London, 1962

SUMMERSON, J. 'The Vision of J. M. Gandy', in *Heavenly Mansions*, London, 1949

SUTTON, T. *The Daniells: artists and travellers*, London, 1954

TWINING, T. *Travels in India a hundred years ago*, London, 1893

VALENTIA, LORD: see ANNESLEY

WATKIN, D. 'Some Dufour Wallpapers: a neo-classical venture into the Picturesque', *Apollo*, June 1967, pp. 432–35

——*Thomas Hope 1769–1831 and the neo-classical idea*, London, 1968

In addition to the publications listed above, much material has been obtained from the India Office Records (Court Minutes, Marine Records, Bengal and Madras European Inhabitants) and European manuscripts, as well as from the Farington Diary typescript in the Prints and Drawings Department of the British Museum. Albums of Press Cuttings in the Victoria and Albert Museum Library and Indian Newspapers in the India Office Library have also been used.

Index

Numerals in roman refer to text pages ('22') or to the captions ('no. 93').
Numerals in *italic* indicate illustrations – on text pages ('*22*'), as black-and-white plates ('*no. 93*'), or colour plates ('*XVI*').